LA FABRICA

THIS IS NOT A HOUSE.

TEXTS BY JULI CAPELLA

RAMÓN ESTEVE

P. 6

OBJECTS LIKE HOUSES

JULI CAPELLA

> *I don't see any difference between architecture and the scale of small objects. It's always architecture.*
>
> Norman Foster

What is the difference between a house and an object? From a creative point of view, regardless of definition, it is scale.

Ramón Esteve emerges on the panorama of Spanish creativity with a particular style that he ingeniously applies to both houses and objects. Following in the tradition of architect designers, he makes his contribution from Valencia with international ambitions. He designed his first piece of furniture in 1996 and did so precisely to furnish one of his houses, as he could not find what he wanted on the market. From then on, his career in the world of design, parallel to and concomitant with his work as an architect, has been swiftly successful and consistently excellent.

Born in Valencia in 1964, he has always lived in Ontinyent, where, even as a child, he displayed an aptitude for handiwork and ingenuity. Drawing is his main expressive tool:

> *As to how my interest in design originated, when I was small, I was already very curious about things. At home, I had a little room where I tested my abilities, dismantled toys and then put others together with various pieces. I did DIY and also made electrical circuits. Later, scale models. I was good at handiwork. But apart from that, I drew all the time when I was a boy. I wasn't a great student, but I never stopped drawing. I've always liked it: I enjoy drawing.*[1]

His inclination was to study fine arts, but he finally matriculated in architecture. His experience at the faculty in Madrid opened up a horizon of knowledge which, when extrapolated to the world of art, was to be the key to his later professional practice. He was suffused with a radical concept of how architecture should be regarded—not as a profession, but as an existential vocation. Figures like Sáenz de Oza and, above all, Professor Paco Alonso, with his singular ideas about what it is to be an architect, prompted him to make both conceptual and tectonic demands upon himself that were to model his defining features.

Esteve's great discovery has been to root his creative potential in geographical and sociocultural coordinates. His contribution is having created a language fed by rationalism that has evolved towards organicism on a human scale, and having made it meet the circumstantial requirements of his operative environment—that is, Valencia and the eastern Mediterranean coast of Spain—while maintaining the ambition of a universal language.

1. Conversation with Juli Capella.

ENLARGING THE SPATIAL EXPERIENCE

How can an architect exert maximum control and offer the greatest possible expression of his creativity? By deciding everything he can. This ranges from the site to the urban setting, including the structures and enclosures, but also the design of the building interiors and, if possible, their furnishings, right down to the door handles and, if he is permitted, the vase and flowers that will decorate the living room, and even the music that will go best with those spaces. In the search for the greatest possible sensory experience for the inhabitant, there is room for designing everything.

In 2015, Esteve presented his doctoral thesis, significantly entitled *La fabricación del interior*, with the subtitle 'Arquitectura y mobiliario en la contemporaneidad'. It is a meticulous and subjective survey of architects' main contributions to the creation of contemporary furnishings, of which they were undoubtedly the pioneers and the protagonists. Beginning with the avant-garde movements of the 1920s, he traces an evolution enriched by the arrival of new materials and technologies, building up to the current typological repertoire of furniture.

The curious thing, however, is that in his own development as a furniture designer, Esteve has followed practically the same itinerary, though not in a linear or mimetic way, but tentatively. That is, in each of his different challenges, whether chairs, tables or lamps, he has raised the most purely conceptual questions of the different 'isms' in the history of design. In this way, he resolves the challenge of the Cantilever chair initiated by Breuer and Stam, and he explores Miesian minimalism, fine-tuning it with metal profiles. He then tones down more uncompromising proposals, traversing an organicism of Aaltian inspiration, though Jacobsen is also present, with close attention paid to wood. And always underlying his work is the holistic, geometricising and integrating approach of Frank Lloyd Wright, though more from the point of view of concept than that of formalisation. In their own way, Esteve's pieces run through the trail left by the great furniture-designing master architects.

His work is therefore also framed by that of Spanish architects who have likewise felt the need to finish their buildings with their own furnishings, from Gaudí and other modernist architects to Luis and Javier Feduchi, the rationalists of GATCPAC, Bonet Castellana, Barba Corsini, Rafael Moneo, and Óscar Tusquets and Lluís Clotet. The last two created the BD production company to make pieces nobody else dared to manufacture, and Esteve launched a similar endeavour.

JULI CAPELLA

FINISHING OFF ARCHITECTURE

Esteve's initial interest was not so much designing furniture for pleasure as finishing off his architectural works. It is important here to mention his brilliant career in his prime occupation. Although it is not the object of this book, which focuses on design, it must be stressed that he has managed to create a remarkable style of his own. It is also imperative to say that his furnishings are still architecture. In fact, they are microarchitectures that fit into the mother architecture of the building. This is stated explicitly in his doctoral thesis:

> *The author approaches furniture design in the conviction that it is necessary for the furnishings to be developed coherently with the space that houses them if the architecture is to fulfil all its sensory potential. This study therefore seeks to elucidate the relationship between furnishing and architecture in such a way that the former acts as a connecting element between a place and the person who inhabits it, amplifying the perception of the habitational experience.*[2]

Scale has always represented an interesting dilemma for artists. On the one hand, size is the first aspect to be taken into consideration. On the other, how it interrelates with the rest of the environment and how far it is possible to extrapolate it. With furnishing, for example, we might regard a table as a small construction with four columns and a flat roof, which is how a child playing underneath it would understand it. The chair is basically a similar undertaking that takes load-bearing capacity into account. Once again, it is a structure with façades and a specific aesthetic and, as in a building, a particular creative process for which the choice of materials and the constructive details that shape it are crucial. In other words, there may, and must be, an interlocking of the two processes, house and object, especially if we want them to live in harmony. From this perspective, rather than creating furniture for his houses, Esteve has taken the radical step of concluding his projects without departing from them, down to the final detail.

Esteve applies the same strategy to interior design, simply extending the architecture to the surfaces, floor, walls and ceiling to create continuity with the exterior. The architecture itself is faced both outside and in. The concept of interior design, usually considered an addition to architecture, is not really even valid here, and far less that of décor, which is totally outside his interest. It is solely a question of the design of the building.

The support of geometry, so clear for an architect, merits special mention in all his work. It is the basis of his investigations and a tool for refined solutions, although he does not allow himself to be enslaved by it. Rather, he plays with it and moulds it towards achieving his objective of 'combining matter and light to transform geometry into emotion'.

2. Ramón Esteve, *La fabricación del interior* (doctoral thesis), 2015.

REPRODUCIBILITY OF THE SINGULAR

Even if a piece of furniture is designed for a specific place, it may well fit into and harmonise with other surroundings. This is the empathetic magic of many pieces that have ended up populating vast territories, despite having been conceived for a particular locale. Mies's Barcelona chair must have been an ephemeral throne in the 1929 pavilion in Barcelona, but it has adapted very well to hotel lobbies and luxurious offices. The *chaise longue* made by Charles and Ray Eames so that the film director Billy Wilder could take a nap during shooting now provides repose in many out-of-the-way places for all sorts of people. They do have to be thin, though.

Esteve's first pieces had that luck. They were appreciated in other settings, and so went into serial production. They achieved this for several reasons, including the facts that they filled a typological gap and were excellently constructed. The principal example of this is Esteve's reinvention of the typology of outdoor furnishings for domestic terraces. Until then, nearly everything had been cheesy or vulgar (except for the Du Champ lounge chair by Clotet and Tusquets, made in *deployé*). Esteve's concepts were so innovative and opportune that a large collection of imitations and copies followed. The genre, however, had by then already been reinvented.

Another important characteristic of his pieces is his command of the material and his way of treating it. Most of the architects of the modern movement showed concern for materials and manufacturing processes, but that interest went into decline among postmodern architects, who sought only form without contributing new principles of construction. Esteve, however, returns to an obsession with detail, thoroughly conversant with modern technologies and skilful and capable when it comes to constructing the piece with different elements.

Since settling into the universe of serial production, his studio has experienced exciting growth, both in the diversification of its design areas and in the ambition with which its collections are completed. Its network of clients has also spread to international production companies ranging from Italy to the United States. The industrial design of furnishings, lighting, or anything else has in turn become a separate department of the studio, no longer restricted to the firm's own collections but still governed by the same concept of formal coherence.

JULI CAPELLA

INVENTING AN ESSENTIALLY MEDITERRANEAN STYLE

Esteve's career is framed within the work of other architects who have gone into design to finish off their buildings, and we have already seen several examples of this. Even though they share this interest, however, the strategies employed are very diverse, as are the formal end products. Each creator gradually configures their own style, seeking to distinguish their work from that of their colleagues. Esteve has also developed a particular style, strictly allied at first to his architectural work but increasingly independent from it as time has gone by.

After twenty-five years of experience, he has consolidated a peculiar style of his own that we might call essentially Mediterranean, timeless and sober. His designs always display a compositional purity of great elegance. Whether the forms are simple or more elaborate and organic, they are always strong and geometrical, and despite their radical aesthetics, they are comfortable and functional—something that is not easy to achieve. There is nothing strident or experimental. His is a national contribution to the most demanding minimalism, far from banal simplicity. Rather than minimalist, his work is better described as essential, harmonious, synthetic and serene. He undoubtedly pursues beauty, a word that does not frighten him. Every new piece has been a challenge met with ingenuity, constructive risk and a professional approach. There is no straw filling or minor work; all his pieces seek excellence in their genesis and synthesis. If not, they are never born. Seeing them gathered here for the first time, they remind us of a large family full of diversity, but with a potent and recognisable DNA. There is no doubt who the father is, although the mother (the producer) may change.

What might Esteve come up with in the future? Considering that he is not yet sixty, and bearing in mind the proverbial longevity of architects and artists, he still has a long way to go. This book reflects upon his work at the apex of his career, but interesting new brainchildren are certain to be in the offing. It should not be forgotten that creative incontinence is another obsessive feature of any self-respecting integral architect.

P. 12

ORIGIN MATERIAL SKILL STYLE CULTURE

RAMÓN ESTEVE

JULI CAPELLA QUIQUE DACOSTA ANTXÓN GÓMEZ TACHY MORA ALBERTO ANAUT : CONVERSATIONS

Ramón Esteve's personality has been shaped over the years in the space between architecture and the creation of its interiors. It is surprising how much he has managed to produce without making too much noise, as he likes his designs to be, and without losing sight of his origin, which has a great deal to do with originality. Touching the material with his hands, like a craftsman always in search of excellence, he has built up experience and expertise in a cycle that ends as it began, converting Na Xemena into Posidonia in the years from 1996 to 2023. While his style does not necessarily have to be recognisable, it is nonetheless perceptible, and it allows us to run smoothly through a chronological survey of his work, which is firmly rooted in the culture of hard work and the lessons of history.

Before looking one by one at those designs, we must get to know the person. One way to do so, and the method chosen here, is to see him reflected in others, conversing with five other figures who form part, each in their own way, of the world of creativity: Juli Capella, architect and populariser of design, and the author of the texts in this publication; Quique Dacosta, a multi-starred chef with whom he shares a love of his land; Antxón Gómez, artistic director and production designer, and a habitual collaborator on nearly all the films of Pedro Almodóvar; Tachy Mora, journalist and exhibition curator, who specialises in design and its trends; and finally Alberto Anaut, who sadly passed away while this publication was at press and founder of La Fábrica, a cultural management firm that reaches beyond the publishing house which has brought out this book.

CONDUCTED BY RAMÓN ÚBEDA (RÚ)

ORIGIN

How do origins influence the work of any architect or designer? First, there is the period of apprenticeship; then, the context of professional development, which is also geographical; and finally, the way the product is exported to other places or cultures which may be very different.

JULI CAPELLA (JC) + RAMÓN ESTEVE (RE)

JC Your origin is Valencia.

RE I was born in Valencia, but I spent nearly all my childhood and youth in Ontinyent, until I went to study architecture. I always say I'm not a desk designer but a street designer, and that's because of my origin. I grew up next to craftsmen, and I was habitually to be found in a carpenter's, locksmith's or marble mason's workshop. A small town gives you very easy access to all that, because everything is close and everyone knows one another. When I saw what was being done in those workshops, a thousand different things occurred to me. Having those infrastructures so close to me proved fundamental, because they are a school.

RÚ The school of the craftsman's trade.

RE When I read the book by the great master Miguel Milá entitled *Lo esencial: el diseño y otras cosas de la vida*, I realised we had lots of things in common. It's not by chance that he's one of my great influences because of the value he attaches to the craftsman and the artisan. It's also true there are designers nowadays who were born in the digital world and still do interesting things.

JC In your case, you had a much more material origin. Are you a good handyman?

RE I've always liked hardware stores. There were several ironmongers in Ontinyent, because there's an important textile industry there. They're not ordinary hardware stores. They look more like warehouses, and you can find everything you want in them, from nuts and bolts to all kinds of machinery. I've always found it inspiring to go and look at tools. Everything is globalised now, but before, if you went to Sweden, Germany or Italy, you found the tools were shaped differently to the ones in Spain. That means that even the design of a tool, whose purpose is purely functional, can also have a cultural component, so I've always found it very interesting to analyse those anonymous designs linked to different cultures.

RÚ I think Juli has a story to tell about that.

JC Many years ago, Achille Castiglioni came to Barcelona for an exhibition we organised during the Design Spring. I asked him what he wanted to see in the city: the Sagrada Familia, the bullring… 'No, no', he said. 'Take me to a hardware store. When I go to a city, it's what I most like to visit'.

RE Even if their function is the same, tools and equipment are different in every culture. I admit it's unusual to arrive in Japan and ask straight off for a hardware store, as you say

Castiglioni also did. My origins as a designer came from there. If I ended up designing furniture, it was because I had been able to get to know the different crafts from the inside. The first collection I did with Gandía Blasco began with steel profiles and perforated sheet metal because I developed it at the locksmith's studio I generally worked with.

Afterwards we moved onto aluminium, and I found solutions that also came from the craftsman's studio for a firm that has no infrastructure or assembly line. I went to a window manufacturer, and with what they did plus an invention of my own, a butt joint, the Na Xemena collection was made, first in aluminium and wood and afterwards with polyethylene. It was then that it proved successful, and we managed to draw attention to outdoor furnishings.

RÚ We're talking about 1996. Na Xemena was really a pioneering proposal, and in a way it's the one that gives this book its purpose, because now it's been brought out again with the name of Posidonia.

RE It's the beginning and the end of a phase we want to show.

JC Tell us about the figures who have most influenced you.

RE The international ones. Through Paco Alonso, I started to discover Sigurd Lewerentz and the Scandinavians, who are the ones who have most influenced me along with Frank Lloyd Wright. My architecture has a lot to do with his organic architecture. Also, Alvar Aalto and Louis Kahn, for their appreciation of history.

JC None of them is Mediterranean.

RE Also, without a doubt, Josep Lluís Sert and José Antoni Coderch. After I did Na Xemena, I went to visit Sert's houses in Ibiza and came away fascinated.

JC The influence of the rationalists can be seen in your works too.

RE Le Corbusier, of course. His last phase. The Maisons Jaoul have influenced some of my projects. Not so much because of the exposed brickwork and the Catalan vault, but through the use of the load-bearing walls and the importance in the design of the carpentry in the large windows.

JC Did you design anything when you were at university?

RE No. It was afterwards that I entered the world of design, knowing hardly anything about it: the Eames and not much else. When I discovered Arne Jacobsen, he became a key referent for me. Of the great masters, I would cite Wright, Mies and also Le Corbusier. All of them did furniture, but the ones who really made transcendent contributions to the world of furnishing were Alvar Aalto and Arne Jacobsen.

RÚ When architects designed.

RE That gave rise to my doctoral thesis, entitled *La fabricación del interior: arquitectura y mobiliario en la contemporaneidad*. All the twentieth century-avant-garde architects were concerned with planning not only the space but also all the elements forming part of it. I regard architecture that way too.

JC Another of your characteristics is that you always plan from the inside out. You make furniture like architecture. Some of your drawings could even represent a building just as easily as a piece of furniture.

RE The Na Xemena collection has the same concept and geometry as a house.

JC You wrote your thesis twenty-five years after studying in Madrid. As soon as you finished, you went back to Ontinyent, and later you ended up in Valencia.

RE The city decants talent, as Lewis Mumford said. I became a teacher at the Architecture School of the UPV, and afterwards I did the doctorate. I work in a city, Valencia, which is the geographical epicentre of my origins. Nowadays, it's true there's no need to be in a big city. You can win the Pritzker Prize while based in Olot, as in the case of RCR, or like Peter Zumthor, who lives and works in a small village in Switzerland, Haldenstein.

JC I'd say there's more merit to that.

RE You can isolate yourself thanks to technology, as we were forced to learn during the pandemic. To plan things, however, I need to keep up personal contacts and be with my team, and I also need surroundings that help you find what you're looking for. You receive gifts from contact with the materials. When you design with a pencil on a desk, you're exerting too much control over what you're doing. There's no chance, no contribution from anything fortuitous. It's vital to generate environments where that experimentation exists and you can find other things you weren't looking for. The internet can't give you that.

JC And people who rely only on the internet end up always doing the same thing once they've left school. What was the origin of your practice in the profession?

RE My first project was a stand for Kodak at the SIMO trade fair, as soon as I finished school. I also did some small interior decorating jobs, like a jeweller's shop for a friend. In fact, when I was starting out in Ontinyent, I was classed as an interior decorator because I had 'good taste'. I wasn't happy about that at first, but it gave me an advantage that's become one of my strengths: starting at the end allowed me to value the detail. If I'd begun my career by working on large projects, I might never have had that contact with the small scale.

RÚ And we all know that 'God is in the details'. Those words are by the writer Gustave Flaubert, although we know them through Mies van der Rohe. Nobody would imagine that the German master drew adornments for a plasterer before joining Peter Behrens's studio.

JC You used to have your studio in the same apartment you lived in. Did you work for anyone before that?

RE I never worked in any studio other than my own. That's both an advantage and an inconvenience. The advantage is that you can shape yourself in your own way, and the inconvenience is that you have to invent things that are already invented, and discover things that are already discovered. In time, I hired consultants to help me learn about the running of other studios, which might have, for example, a CEO, a communications department, and so on.

RÚ Those are things they don't teach you at school.

RE The negative thing about schools is that they're machines for generating prejudices transmitted by the teachers themselves, and I say this having been a teacher for a time. Without meaning to, obviously, they transmit their vision to you, and with it their fears, while you remain unaware that it's just their personal vision. You need some time to develop before you're able to create your own independent vision of architecture and design. On the other hand, let's be fair, universities also teach you some very good things. For me, there are two things that are the most important of all. One is consistency, and I learned that from Paco Alonso, a person who practised what he preached. The second, besides all the theoretical knowledge of the profession, is what you learn from your colleagues. That's something you can only find at school, because you're living with people who are searching for the same thing. Those are two extremely important experiences that a purely digital environment today can't give you, either. Cohabitation and personal contact form part of the learning process.

JC What was your final project for graduation?

RE A housing estate in Florida, where I mixed dwellings with small studio industries, something which might be contemporary today if you think of the 'makers' and how that movement is evolving. It's a lifestyle of mediaeval origin that lasted up to the Industrial Revolution. My studio is like that. The living quarters are upstairs, and the workspace downstairs.

It's important to understand that from the creative point of view, as a designer, my studio is closer to a craftsman's workshop than a firm, even if it undoubtedly is one. However, for the studio to function as a brand, we have the figure of Juan Ferrero, who first came in as a trainee, ended up as a partner, and is now the CEO. He has helped me structure the studio as it is now. I have a great team, and I need to feel its complicity and share my passion for architecture and design with it.

JC Did you ever want to be an entrepreneur so as to produce your designs?

RE I tried, but it didn't work, because business management didn't motivate me. Or because what I would really like to have done is what was achieved by Terence Conran or Tom Dixon, who have managed to create not only objects or architecture but whole environments linked to a lifestyle.

Different historical moments, which have to do with a particular context, also generate an aesthetic, which is a way of seeing the world. That's why it's so important that what you design should owe itself to that moment.

JC It's clear that your referent is universal culture, so we could say it's not your Valencian surroundings.

RE With time, I'm discovering all the contemporary design culture there is in Valencia. It didn't influence me at first, although I now form part of it in some way. Actually, I think the true impact came from Mediterranean culture, which involves a wider scope in both a historical and a geographical sense.

(MEDITERRANEAN)

RÚ Obviously, the Mediterranean has also influenced you.

RE It's not that it influences me. It's in my blood.

JC With your houses, you've created a kind of Mediterranean imaginary.

RE It was already there. The masonry I use, with its large sections of wall, comes from the *masías*, the Catalan farmhouses. Vernacular Mediterranean architecture has also been a point of reference for me. So too are certain popular and anonymous objects to be found in it: utensils of wood, pottery or zinc-plated steel.

JC You said yourself that inspiration is living every day and noticing everything. You're one of those designers who work full time. There are some who 'work as' and some, as in your case, who 'are'.

ORIGIN

RE I'm always asked when I switch off, and I always answer by asking why I should want to switch off. Sometimes I'm talking to someone and my mind wanders off because I've seen something that inspires me, that attracts me, and I start thinking of some project.

JC I generally explain that one day I put on my designer's spectacles and I've never been able to take them off since then. It's awful, dangerous even, because you're tuned in all day. You're constantly scanning everything you see.

RE The structure of a designer is based first and foremost on training. Where does the inspiration come from? Architecture and design. Of the past? Of the immediate past and the near future. You put what you saw three minutes ago together with the baggage that comes from your training, and you develop it to take a step forward.

On the other hand, I can say that I've been to see Chichén Itzá, the Pyramid of Khafre and the Pantheon of Agrippa, and that they situate you in history and help you relativise the present. When it comes to planning, however, I'm much more inspired by a house by Coderch or any everyday and anonymous object that draws my attention. Andy Warhol used to say that what he did was to copy the mediocre and do it better. It might sound pretentious, but the fact is that sometimes you can get good ideas from things that are no good. As you go around with that attitude you were commenting on of being constantly on the alert, you can get material from anywhere.

JC Picasso went further and supposedly said that 'good artists copy, the great steal'. But that's another discussion.

(SHADOW)

RE It's true that I take influences from Nordic architecture to make it Mediterranean. I design large windows behind large shadows.

JC To adapt to the climate.

RE When there was still no bioclimatic consciousness, I was already using thermal inertias, crossed ventilations and shadows in front of the glass. My first houses didn't need air conditioning.

JC Your outdoor furnishings also seek shade. Or shelter.

RE The daybeds. I eased quite naturally into designing outdoor furnishings. In fact, I've been catalogued within the speciality. What I really did was to reproduce the interior programme of the house on the exterior. Life on the Mediterranean, which has a benign climate nearly all the year round, allows you to cook outside and have your living room on the porch.

JC And to have a siesta.

RE It's one of the most wonderful moments you can have, to be enjoyed after reading a book, when there's a little breeze. I also love living and relating to others, which is something we tend to do outdoors in our culture.

JC Your sofas are always designed with that in mind. A siesta or a party.

RE I was one of those who studied hard all year and then, no matter how many subjects I had left, I would pass them all the following year. The summer was sacred. I've always liked going out, and I took my fun as seriously as my studies. The Mediterranean has that touch of hedonism that invites you to enjoy yourself. The ludic part of life is fundamental.

MATERIAL

For some people, that ludic and enjoyable part of life is concentrated in the stomach. Designing and cooking have a lot in common. The material of which a designer is made is not very different from what makes up a chef: tradition, authenticity, creativity, quality…

QUIQUE DACOSTA (QD) + RAMÓN ESTEVE (RE)

RE There's a parallel between the two disciplines of gastronomy and fine design, both of which have evolved exponentially in recent years. First designers emerged in the eighties, and then came the chefs, who have given us a lesson as a professional group. One proof of this evolution is that no chef now opens a restaurant without attaching to the furnishing and décor the importance they merit. The proposal is not in the dish alone.

QD And we might consider there's no point in creating a traditional menu with futurist furnishings, or an avant-garde cuisine with classical furniture. It's a question of trying to give a bit of consistency to the narrative of your work, but it's not dogma. The most modern and disruptive restaurant in the world of cuisine over the last thirty years is El Bulli, which displayed extreme creativity in an old Catalan farmhouse, with the chairs, the beams, the windows and the floors it already had in it.

RÚ And they were never changed.

QD An added value was simply given in terms of infrastructure and technology to the cuisine, which was really the heart of the project. But where the dining-room was concerned…

RÚ There's always an exception that proves the rule.

QD What they were doing in the kitchen was so powerful that everything else was pushed a long way into the background. That was the most absolute avant-garde. For those of us who shared that time with it and were doing the same kind of thing, it was a referent for a movement that remains active and which we've continued.

RÚ They were the first to produce a book on cooking that was well photographed and well designed.

QD *El Bulli: el sabor del Mediterráneo* was the title of that first book.

RE It's true there was a giant leap forward with El Bulli, as there was with architecture and design at the start of the twentieth century. I don't know whether there was some gastronomic revolution linked to culture at that time. When did what we might call the more 'cultured' cuisine begin?

QD That happened in France. When they cut off the king's and queen's heads and all the aristocrats' chefs left the palaces, they became independent and started to open restaurants.

RE And to work for the new bourgeoisie.

QD They started to sublimate the very way people ate. Although that probably already began in the time of ancient Rome.

RE We turn it almost into a performance and make it something that transcends the food itself. When you go to eat at any kind of restaurant, it's an experience, good or bad. I'm talking about a consciously designed experience. I wonder if the same thing happens as with objects. They've existed since the beginnings of mankind, as each civilisation produces its own, but there comes a time when they start to be made and designed deliberately. As with the Bauhaus, it's the moment when the craftsman, the designer and the artist come together, and the whole revolution dates from then on. Is there a school like the Bauhaus in cuisine?

(REVOLUTION)

QD Yes. In the nineteenth century, César Ritz invented a new way of understanding hostelry. He started to incorporate running water, heating and electricity, sanitary devices which were then considered an extreme luxury. He also introduced materials like marble and stone to the bathrooms, which until then had generally been wooden and carpeted. He revolutionised that world with a whole range of details, and even managed to sell them to the Carlton family, who created the Ritz-Carlton hotels. And he did the same thing for restaurants by forming an association with Auguste Escoffier, the father of a modern gastronomy developed from traditional cuisine. Later, in the seventies, *nouvelle cuisine* arrived to revolutionise those recipes through creativity. We are the children of that movement.

RÚ César Ritz is said to have designed his furnishings, or to have had them designed, smaller than usual so that the rooms would appear bigger. Escoffier, for his part, was the inventor of the menu *à la carte* in restaurants.

QD *Nouvelle cuisine* had several outstanding figures, such as Michel Guérard, the Troisgros brothers and Paul Bocuse, who was probably not the best or most creative of them all, but was certainly the leader of the movement and its centre of media attention. Bocuse had a list of commandments which largely remain valid today. If we had to draw up ten commandments for contemporary Spanish *haute cuisine*, we would probably include many of his.

RÚ Where's the difference, then?

QD Besides the concepts that enshrine the values of *haute cuisine*, which are creativity, knowledge, territory, product and skill, a new one has been added—play. Suddenly, something appears on the scene that had never been envisaged before: the fact that you can play at table. And you start, for example, to eat with your hands when everything before was very academic, especially *haute cuisine*. That play, approached from a serious point of view rather than a flippant or naive one, opens up new possibilities, since questions like cuisine and territory had already been addressed by that generation in France and those who came afterwards in Spain, Italy or England, who were their direct heirs.

RE The word 'play' also forms part of that definition given by Le Corbusier: 'Architecture is the masterly, correct and magnificent play of masses brought together in light.' It's something aleatory, yet bound by certain rules that leave room for creativity and spontaneity. You can adopt or establish those rules yourself; that's another possibility. Whenever the rules are broken, a new order appears. That happens in general with any movement. In contemporary art, for instance, one point of rupture with preceding movements was Dadaism, which broke away from all the traditional rules of classical art to open up a new path. I think something along similar lines is happening to you in cuisine.

QD In our case, those historic moments aren't in the cookery books, because the language with which cooks write their personal history crystallises in recipes, which are the musical scores of chefs. The history of gastronomy is written in the meantime by critics or journalists who date and document events. On the other hand, it's also true that gastronomic movements don't follow one another in succession. For example, the Spanish avant-garde is in progress while *Nouvelle Cuisine* continues to evolve. In the midst of all this, naturalism appears, a language that has a great deal to do with architecture and landscaping. It represents a series of values attached to all that has come before, but it radically discards things like proteins of animal origin or fats.

RE Inevitably, there are parallels between the concerns that arise in design and gastronomy. In design, the Bauhaus was a catalyst and a centre of convergence.

RÚ Now resuscitated as the New European Bauhaus, its main objectives include 'mobilizing designers, architects, engineers, scientists, students and creative minds of all disciplines to reimagine a sustainable life.' I suppose those creative minds include chefs.

QD In cuisine, there hasn't been an academy, but there have been places where knowledge has been concentrated and imparted. It's happened in Spain, but only twenty years ago.

RE Things are very dispersed. In fact, the great merit of a movement like the Bauhaus was that it catalysed all that was happening in the worlds of art, design and architecture at that time. Photography helped it reach broader awareness by documenting all the effort that was made. From what I see, it's the same thing as El Bulli Foundation has achieved: acting as a point of convergence for *haute cuisine* and ensuring visibility for its creations.

QD We've all worked on spreading the word, though what Ferran Adrià does is catalogue. If there's one thing that distinguishes Spanish cuisine from the rest in terms of style, it's creativity, the ability to create new dishes, new tendencies, new forms and techniques applied to the products resulting in new ways forward. Because he's close to art, Ferran realises that any painter has his or her work catalogued, and he's starting to do the same.

RE That work of documentation, compiling the information and archiving it for subsequent diffusion, has been of key importance, as cuisine is an ephemeral thing that gets dispersed. That's given you transcendence.

QD To my mind, the only way a cook can become transcendent is by training others and creating equals. We live in a world where nobody remembers anyone. The king is dead, long live the king. Everything gets forgotten very fast.

RE Knowledge is originated by documenting it in books. The same is true of objects. They're just there until someone photographs them and gives them a value. Another important thing you chefs have done, and which also has a parallel in the world of design, is to generate a personality along the lines of a rock star. Both of us are nearly in the world of show business, whereas there were no such figures in the profession before. It's a major leap to begin to have visibility and move in the world of communication.

QD Now we understand that knowledge is donated, which means a mental and intellectual opening for the artisan who decides to do so.

RE And if not, it doesn't transcend. Those recipes are going to be your true bequest. That's going to be your great contribution, because a dish, when all's said and done, gets eaten up.

(CREATIVITY)

QD For example, I'm the intellectual property holder of landscape cuisine. The first landscape appeared in 2003, and I see it as a natural evolution of the cuisine of the *terroir*. However, it represents the territory I want to show in the dish in a graphic and abstract way, not figuratively. Since then, hundreds or thousands of chefs around the world have done or are doing something similar to that, which has a creator with no *carte blanche*, no brand, nothing. All you can do is spread the news quickly, because in such a fast-moving world as ours, it's sometimes difficult to prove it's yours.

RE The legislation on designer goods makes it more difficult for people to copy you, but architecture is a completely open field. You can copy your heart out, and it's very difficult to do anything about it.

RÚ That's why the important thing in every case is to define each personality, so it can be certified in some way that it was you who created it.

QD At this stage in the game, nearly everyone knows or recognises that we chefs are creators. I might also consider us as designers, but what about the bad reputation 'designer cuisine' has acquired? If you put it on your door, you're dead.

RE Of course, because it's been abused in the worst sense of the word. For me, a good design is one that doesn't look as though it's been designed. It's there, without shouting. Good design isn't perceptible, it's in harmony with its context while it's fulfilling its function. Its beauty lies in the conscious humility that allows it to exist and serve us sustainably in the long term. I think excesses are always a bad thing. The word 'design' is despised because of abuse, but it's still the *raison d'être* of nearly everything. There's nothing that isn't designed. I think it's clear in the case of cuisine. Behind every dish, it's crucial for there to be a good composition. The problem might arise when the composition can't be eaten, when it's purely decorative. The key is to find what is essential in any field: the balance between form and depth, between design and content.

RÚ There's good design and bad design, but design is everything. The problem is we haven't managed to communicate that to people. I've been trying for forty years, and I'm still occasionally asked in interviews: 'How would you define design?'

RE I was asked that, and I came off well with this definition from Google: 'Creative activity whose purpose is to plan objects that are useful and aesthetic.' Now that's very clear! We can use it as a simple way to distinguish what's well designed from what isn't. It must be beautiful and useful. On occasions, I've asked myself these questions: why, how and what for. The why responds to the function, the prime objective of an object. The how responds to all the processes, artisanal or industrial. And the what for has to do with transcendence. Besides serving and being, the object has to create an emotional connection with whoever's using it. That's where its beauty resides. It's a transcendental question that can be applied to nearly all disciplines.

RÚ To say that a chair is a designer object is like calling a dish gastronomy. No, this dish was made by a cook. Everything is gastronomy—the 'art of preparing a good meal', as the dictionary of the Spanish Academy also defines it—from the humblest cooking to what you do.

RE People like to classify. I'll probably repeat more than once during this conversation that there are two architectures, vernacular and cultured. The rest is speculation: heaps of bricks or tiles that cover you, but which don't have that emotional or cultural side. The same is true of cuisine. On the one hand, you have vernacular cooking, which is cultural and belongs to a society. On the other, you have what is made by an individual, a creator, which obviously belongs to a specific civilisation and period, but has the capacity to transmit emotions and culture through an object or a space. And there are only those two variants. The rest are things, not designs.

QD In my world, it would be like calling what McDonald's does cuisine.

RE Exactly.

QD Part of the problem is that everything gets called a restaurant, including a McDonald's. And there's a transformation of the product there: food gets grilled and heated, tomatoes get sliced, sauces get put on top… There comes a point when it also needs to be clarified whether the term 'restaurant', the term 'architect' and the term 'design' really define us all. *Chef* is a word with a lot of peculiarities, but there's a hint of cultural reflection, of intentions…

RÚ Of creativity, in this case.

RE Yes, but what is creativity? Here we're moving onto concepts that are essential, because where's the cut-off point? In other words, creativity is everything. In this case too, there's good and bad.

QD There's creativity when there's an intention to create something new. Speaking from my sector, the movement in Spanish cuisine was initially marked by distancing itself from France and *nouvelle cuisine*. Evidently, we're the heirs to that cuisine, but if we want independence and our own status, we have to leave those dogmas behind, even if they're the basis of our history. From that point, you start to pick up the concept of *auteur cuisine*, which is a term currently used in creative cuisine that allows you not only to be the author of your work, but to actually create something, even to be disruptive in the search for what you're going to do. Obviously, you can never be completely disruptive, because in your case, you have to keep setting the concrete inside a formwork. We have to grill, roast, poach, cook, boil… And that's much older than all of us put together.

RE This whole Spanish movement is no more than thirty years old.

RÚ About the same as what we might call 'new Spanish design'.

(RESPECT)

QD A very short time, because the book on El Bulli we were mentioning earlier came out in 1992. But just think that Juan Mari Arzak and Pedro Subijana were there before Adrià.

RE Arzak and Subijana do hail from French influence.

QD But they set something of a mark on the first glimmer of creative intentions and *auteur* cuisine when they said, 'All right, but I'm a Basque.'

RE Because besides cultural influence, there's territorial influence too.

QD The Basque Country, Catalonia and Madrid have certain differences. Basque cuisine, both traditional and creative, had those first leaders beginning with Luis Irízar, who died at the age of almost ninety. Catalan cuisine is both popular and bourgeois. And Madrid crystallised into a setting where this new cuisine could happen, as it needs not only a cultured society but a society that can afford it.

(QUALITY)

QD I don't know if it's possible in your field, but in mine, you can't have an important project without quality. I can't cook with bad ingredients. My basic material can't be bad, and I don't know if it's possible to make wonderful architecture when the material is bad.

RE If we're talking about bad materials, no. But it doesn't necessarily have to be the most expensive, either. We live in a part of the world where fruit and vegetables are very good and cheap. Compare it, for example, with the United States, where fresh produce and greens are more expensive than they are here, or with the fruit stalls in Japan, laid out as if they were jewelleries. We're lucky enough to have a wide variety of local produce. The region of Valencia has a semi-tropical climate where you can plant practically anything and make it work—don't forget that the Borgias made their fortune with sugar cane. I remember that the first time I went to Galicia, many years ago, my friends had never eaten an artichoke or an aubergine because they didn't grow there. You cooks are in an environment with a large amount of local produce of stunning quality and diversity.

QD Of course.

RE It's your palette of materials, the equivalent of what I need to produce my designs. There's a great similarity, because I've always designed on the basis of infrastructures and materials that were close at hand, and which I've tried to understand and bring under control so as to make viable proposals. I imagine that's your case too.

MATERIAL

QD I'd say that 80% of the ingredients I cook weren't in the *haute cuisine* books that inspired me to be the chef I am today.

RE Because those ingredients were already there, in our culture, and they were already superb. You've had the ability to incorporate them to *haute cuisine*. Like Dénia prawns, which you've raised to the highest possible level.

QD *Haute cuisine* dealt with certain products without ever having looked towards this part of the Mediterranean or this area in particular. I understand, however, that regardless of the sources I draw from, whether they're culinary, cultural or artistic, the client who comes here from any other part of the world wants to feel that they're really in the region of Valencia. It's all right for me to represent the territory on the table like that, but it's different if you go to Madrid, New York or London, which are open and cosmopolitan cities that might be 80 kilometres away from the nearest market garden or livestock farm, or 550 kilometres from the sea.

(TRADITION)

RE We Spaniards are culturally accustomed to eating well, as is true of every country with thousands of years of history. I'm talking about taste and quality, not about *haute cuisine*, which is something new because it hasn't been available for that long, and certainly not about its democratisation, which, as in the case of design, is very recent. Spain has an extraordinary and culturally diverse tradition that has long been isolated owing to the country's mountainous geography. This has led to a very varied popular gastronomy with highly differentiated areas.

QD If you go over the map from north to south, from Arzak to Ángel León, you find they're completely different. It's values that unite us. There's always been an appeal to knowledge of tradition, to experience, and of course to quality, but thirty-six years ago, which is the time I've been in the profession, we probably wouldn't have been talking about sustainability as naturally as we do today, or with the same awareness.

(TECHNOLOGY)

RÚ Your cuisine is also associated with technology.

QD But it hasn't contributed an added value. In the cuisine of Quique Dacosta or of Martín Berasategui, no machine has appeared in the last twenty-five years that's proved disruptive enough to generate a paradigm of movement, which may well often be of help, technologically, in your sector, but in ours…

RE It's curious. In architecture, it does help a great deal, and in design as well, very much indeed. Technology has a direct influence. From the technology of materials to the complexity of modern installations.

QD And it has its uses for us too. What's happened is that the oven, which already existed, is now more perfect.

RE And the vacuum?

QD Vacuum cooking was already in the kitchen twenty-five or thirty years ago. Low temperature was there too. We had lyophilisation, induction and the microwave. The Thermomix, as an apparatus, is a blender that heats things up. Technology has contributed relatively little. It helps us come a bit nearer perfection, and to control the processes a little more closely. Now we've seen the appearance of a new technology consisting of printers of edible materials, like paper and so forth, but it's almost decorative, like the frame on a picture.

RE In design, as in architecture, the change has rather been one of concept, of the approach to creativity. Modernity has to do with a new way of confronting the problem and seeing the world. And that, of course, is not always brought about by technology. A good example is Stravinsky, who made contemporary music with 18th-century instruments.

QD Traditionally, cream was put in a siphon. And if I put in mashed potato, will the starch be able to sustain the air collected by the fat when you put in the carbon dioxide? Now that's a chef who thinks. I'm a chef who thinks. If you asked me which cooking technique I would have liked to have invented, I'd say puff pastry.

RÚ Puff pastry?

QD Behind puff pastry, there's someone who makes a dough, adds butter, folds it in a particular way so that the air doesn't escape, and then puts those layers in the oven. The buttermilk then tries to evaporate, and that is what pushes up the layers, making everything rise. Now there is someone who thinks. It isn't known who it was or how long ago. There are recipes that document it two or three hundred years ago. It's something vernacular which, when all is said and done, belongs to everyone. It can be used for sweet or savoury food, and it can represent French *haute cuisine* or at the same time be used to make the most horrible buns you can find in the worst airport in the universe. That would be the technique I'd have liked to invent.

RÚ I would have chosen the stuffed olive.

QD That's a good invention too.

RÚ And it can be produced serially. There's a fundamental difference between these two creative professions. The designer can create, for example, a chair which is then produced industrially and can be sold anywhere in the world. By contrast, anything created by the chef has to be reproduced by hand every day, as though it were a work of art.

QD Every day and on every table. What I do is cookery, and I don't consider myself an artist, no matter what I drink from or what I feed off. And not only in the place where I work every day. I have eleven other restaurants as well.

RE A designer isn't necessarily an artist, either. Wanting to design as if you were an artist, or thinking you are an artist, is something I don't go along with. I prefer to think of myself as a craftsman with a particular way of doing things, and whose creations occasionally go further than what they basically are. Art has many definitions. One of them is the creation of something with no practical use. However, it's true that there's a part of what might be called art that transcends utility, perhaps because even if it is useful, it has the ability to connect with the emotions.

QD And food, when all's said and done, has to nourish you. That's a proactive principle.

RÚ Carlos Rolando used to say that the difference between a designer and an artist is that designers know where their next meal is going to come from.

RE That's amusing. Louis Kahn illustrated it by saying that an artist can make a cannon with square wheels to demonstrate how absurd and senseless war is, but a designer has to make a cannon with round wheels because it has to roll. That's the difference. In the kitchen, an artist can put on a senseless performance, but you have to make something that people can eat. The artist can make you feel as though you've been turned inside out, but the designer can't do that. But that doesn't make it less of a work of art. For me, art is what transforms the material into the immaterial, the tangible into the intangible. That is, art has the capacity to turn ordinary and unimportant materials into objects of value. What's the value of the paint with which *Las meninas* is painted? Hardly anything, and yet it's a creation of incalculable value because of what it represents and conveys. Here we perceive that transcendence from the material to the spiritual. That would be the question. You, from the world of cuisine—and that's why we're here—have managed to transcend the food itself to reach the world of emotion.

(UNIVERSAL)

RÚ In some cases, that emotion is universal. When you take what you've made here and you export it, does it work? Because it doesn't always work.

QD That limits it a great deal, but there comes a moment when I understand where my cuisine stands from a creative perspective. Mercat Bar, Vuelve Carolina, Llisa Negra and El Poblet embrace the same creative values, but adapted to other business models regulated by the same concepts.

RÚ Those you've mentioned are all in the same city. But what if you leave the country?

RE You have a rice restaurant in London. Is it difficult to make a good rice dish in London?

QD As hard as in Valencia.

RÚ Ramón's designs sell just as well in Valencia as in Singapore?

RE There are pieces that are very successful in a particular country. When I have to design for the Americans, I'm always thinking of large pieces because they have a lot more space. Something as simple as that. There may be certain peculiarities, yes, but they're very few. Suddenly, a culture demands more from you because you connect more with its desires, values or customs than for any other reason. Evidently, though, it's much easier to design a piece of furniture that will go nearly anywhere than to offer a menu that will be to everyone's taste.

SKILL

Time is the other great difference between the work of an industrial designer and that of a chef. The dish remains, but what it contains is ephemeral. A production designer moves on the same plane when working for cinema or advertising. In both reality and fiction, professional skill is necessary to stand out from the rest.

ANTXÓN GÓMEZ (AG) + RAMÓN ESTEVE (RE)

AG I work with totally different parameters, but I think this conversation may be fun because they're the parameters of the ephemeral, which also apply to cooking.

RE At the beginning I explained that I started by doing stands, which are ephemeral architecture.

RÚ In your early days, Antxón, there were no restaurants, but there were a few bars.

AG I started out in advertising, but I trained as a chemist. In fact, I loved chemistry and got as far as the fifth year of my degree course. But then a friend suddenly came to my house one day looking for people to lend him a hand with making a commercial. I had just come from an explanation of the atom, I remember it perfectly, but I couldn't see how I could help him. He said to me: 'Your house is very nice.' At that time, I used to hunt for things in the flea market, especially lamps. It's a weakness of mine and I've always liked it, I don't know why. And I said to him: 'Well, all right, stay to dinner.' Since then, he's always reminded me that the potato omelette I made him and the décor of my house were decisive.

RE And you were a hair's breadth from becoming a cook.

AG I love cooking.

RÚ Who was that friend?

AG It was Luis Calvo, a friend from Madrid who afterwards produced Pedro Almodóvar's second film, *Dark Habits*, made in 1983. He got me into this, and I started to do one commercial, then another, then another… Later, I moved on to bars.

RE Which bars have you done?

AG Zig Zag, a legendary bar of the eighties in Barcelona, which I designed together with Guillem Bonet, Alicia Núñez and Ramón Oliva. It won us a FAD Prize for Interior Design, which was important in those days. Then I was a founding partner of the discotheque Otto Zutz.

RE I think it's one of the prettiest discotheques ever made. I was fascinated. In terms of design, it was stunning. That industrial vision, that scenography, that lighting… Because it wasn't grungy disco lighting, it was mysterious and suggestive, like the underground scene of the time.

AG Alicia Núñez did that with Guillem Bonet. I wasn't a part of it. I think it was him who proposed that mural, also legendary, painted by Vicenç Viaplana.

RE And why the name of Otto Zutz?

AG Now, the name is mine. I remember that precisely Guillermo, Alicia and I were coming back one night from dinner, and we wondered, 'What shall we call it?' There was a German optician's on the corner where we had the Zig Zag that was called Otto Zutz. It drew my attention because it was almost a palindrome and lent itself to possibilities. We could say it was the name of a German partner who had put up the money, to throw people off the track. Anyway, the name stuck from that moment on, and the optician either never found out or was a Nazi refugee, because he never said a word.

RE I've designed bars too. One was called Luna, in Ontinyent. Afterwards, a few years ago, I did a restaurant for a chef who was a friend of mine, the Bouet, which has an industrial aesthetic.

(EXPERIENCE)

RÚ Let's talk about experience within the profession. Antxón, how many commercials or adverts have you done?

AG I calculated one day that the figure must be around seven hundred. If we're talking about films, I've done twenty-four.

RE What madness! Now that's experience.

AG What's more, I end up getting into other setups. All ephemeral, like what we've being doing for five years at Utopia Markets. It's a poetry, illustration and photography market where the interesting thing is that the artists themselves are there attending to people.

RÚ And it's been a huge success, proving you can do other things that also fulfil you and don't necessarily have anything to do with your daily professional activity. I'd even say it's to be recommended.

AG For example, we decided to do this altruistically, without charging anything, because we liked the idea of doing something fun and entertaining for the city in a venue we liked very much. So we got down to it, designed some cheap stands, and that was what it was all about. I had the idea for the poetry, but we decided to start with photography because it had more of a pull. We're very multidisciplinary. We'll get into anything.

RE Besides, the interesting thing about this transversality across every profession is that it's something that recurs in every discipline. You draw from one thing to produce another.

AG Certainly, because eventually, as you say, we ended up designing the furnishings. I've looked so often for a piece of furniture without finding it anywhere, and ended up making something myself that worked for me. In our profession, we're driven by necessity. There's one part that's visual and another that's narrative. If you need the actors to move in a space that they have to use in a particular way, you have to get things transformed into what you need.

RE Because things tell stories too. Today, there's an implicit language in any display that's unconscious, but which is there and can be read. It's like the semiotics of objects.

AG It's because we're narrative beings.

RE The fact that you choose or design objects in a particular way already tells us something.

AG Not just objects themselves, but also the space. In cinema, we need spaces to tell us things. How the person who inhabits them lives, right down to the last detail. If he or she is dirty or clean, and so on. It's a process you have to work towards, because sometimes it's not clearly limited. If the director has a vague idea, you have to dig a bit to get something out of them that not even they know they want.

RE You know how to make objects speak.

AG Of course, it has to be that way. That's why I say we're totally narrative. Why does the character have that glass and not another one? Where has it come from? Does it have a story behind it? We need all those things.

RE And if something is very clean, it comes across as artificial. When you see old movies, you don't believe them because they're so clean.

AG The camera cleans, and it tends to clean a lot. Everything then looks kind of unreal. That's why we make heaps of architectural mistakes when we build our sets. We have to make them on purpose.

RE What?

AG Yes, because a two-metre-high wall where nothing is happening looks tremendously boring when seen through a camera. Something has to be done, like putting in a drainpipe, even though there's no point to it, or a girder, even if it's not supporting anything.

RE To give it texture.

AG That's right. But I also think we need to make those mistakes on the set because real life isn't so perfect. We need the life of that place, even if it's unreal, to be an accumulative life: one person bought it, another refurbished it, and a third one lives in it.

RE It's not habitual for something to be so well thought out. Usually, it's time that's created various strata, and in the end it becomes inhabitable owing to that very accumulation of layers.

AG And those layers often aren't even the result of someone's will. That imperfection, that wall which isn't vertical… I've always had an obsession with decentring things. Yesterday I was with the carpenter, and I said to him: 'Don't you dare do it so well. It's so perfect I don't believe it.' Because it has to be wrong so that people will believe in it.

RÚ You 'worsen' it.

RE It's the beauty of imperfection that we find in the Japanese philosophy of *wabi-sabi*. In architecture, I always use materials like stone, which already have an age that enriches them. People are obsessed with things not getting spoilt. When they say, 'But wood spoils', I answer, 'But I want it to spoil'. We have to accept the passage of time in the objects around us. There's a certain beauty that comes of aging. I like to plan with the idea that the passage of time is going to favour the project, not the contrary.

AG That's what we're constantly searching for in cinema. One day, I remember, we were building the sets for a film in Puerto Rico. I said to the builder, 'That's all right, quite good, but have you got a jeep?' So I took the jeep, tied it to the house, and started to pull. As soon as it was out of joint, I thought, 'Now it really is perfect'.

RÚ Was that Steven Soderbergh's film on Che Guevara?

AG Yes, the one starring Benicio del Toro. We built more than you can possibly imagine. But I'm speaking from what happens to be my area. I'm not an architect, but I've always thought an architect should have more freedom than we do. We have a script, and we go with the script.

RE In the end, though, you somehow make it your own. When I'm designing a house, I'm really creating a stage setting so that some people can inhabit it. Beforehand, you try to get to know them and even spend some time sharing their life. In my case, it's my architectural vision of some clients' lifestyle. You make your version of what the director tells you to do.

AG Yes, but in my case, it's ultimately the director who's in charge. You can make your version and be as imaginative as you like, but if they tell you, 'I don't like it in green', then we change colour.

RE Clients must always be listened to, because their voice is important for achieving a good result. There's a question of identity. The client has to identify with the project and see themselves reflected in my way of making architecture. What I want is for there to be coherence, an underlying narrative and an identity. A good client tells you what they want and what they need, but then lets you do it your own way. A good director probably does the same.

AG There are all sorts. The only thing Soderbergh said to me, for example, was, 'I'd like there to be no blue colour in the movie'. All the rest was up to me. On the other hand, Pedro Almodóvar is the opposite: 'I'm going to bring this from home...'

RÚ He chooses your furniture for you.

AG Not just the furniture. Everything. With Pedro, it's got to look as though he's done it all himself. That's extremely important, and it's the way it should be done.

RE That happens. In architecture, the truth is that the more freedom the client gives you, and the more they trust you, the better the project. In design, you start with a commission from a brand that already has its identity. You have to understand it, connect with it, and propose something that will be both yours and that brand's. That point can come in everything you do in this life. You brush up against egos everywhere and in every profession. Knowing how to handle other people's egos is crucial for being able to do things in life.

AG To handle other people's egos, you have to leave your own at home.

RÚ You don't seem to have an ego at all.

RE He has one, but the thing is that he knows how to manage it. In my case, as a designer and an architect, I provide the ideas, but the manufacturing is done by someone else. Unlike a painter or a sculptor, all of us have to go through others and work with others. For that reason, either you have a capacity for empathy and the ability to manage egos or you don't succeed in getting anything done. Architectural projects have a choral nature, and a group of people is necessary to bring them to a conclusion. It's essential to know how to connect with them and motivate them.

AG Above all because there are directors who are more important even than the actors. People don't say, 'Have you seen the movie by such-and-such an actor?' No, they say, 'Have you seen the Almodóvar movie?' There's an inversion of values. Some people achieve that. A film by Tarantino is a film by Tarantino, and then there's a list of people. The director's stamp goes ahead of them all.

(CONSTANCY)

RÚ You must also have the professional skill to understand what that director wants. How many years have you been working with Pedro?

AG Twenty-seven.

RE That's a tremendously long time.

AG I think it has to do with the client's thinking: 'My problem is already solved. Why complicate things?'

RÚ We congratulate you on your modesty, but it's obvious he appreciates a certain way of going about things that quite closely resembles the way Ramón designs.

RE I try to design sober things that are almost anonymous, that don't seem to have anyone behind them.

AG We live off appearance and, what's more, off an appearance that mustn't be noticed. I always say that the work of a good art director in cinema is the kind that's not noticeable. Our intervention is sometimes so subtle that it can even look as though you haven't done anything at all.

RE The magic is there. That's the beauty of things which are designed without being noticed, the things which only the passage of time or an attentive gaze can reveal in their normality. The search for the universal in the everyday.

AG One entertaining thing we have in cinema is the false appearance of materials. From giant rocks made of plaster to leather that's not leather or wood that's not wood. It's astonishing how much we're able to deceive the eye. Almost as astonishing as how fleeting it all is. It never ceases to surprise me how that ability to create or recreate wonderful spaces and wonderful dreams has such a short expiry date. You can build a ranch in the middle of a plain in Toledo—the house, the stable, the wind pump, the water tank, the horses and everything—and you see it there and say, 'That's great!' But in two days' time, it has to be dismantled.

P. 36

(CHARACTER)

RÚ And you start all over again somewhere else. You're from the north. Were you influenced by living on the Mediterranean?

AG I'm from San Sebastián, and I came from another sea—a wild one, with waves. As Georges Bataille said, 'from a sea that masturbates'. I found this one unexciting, and I didn't understand it. But one day I realised it was a trading sea, totally different from the one in the north, where the fishermen used to take their lives in their hands with the whales and their rowing boats. The Mediterranean is a conversational sea.

RE It's a friendly sea. And a hedonistic one. Enjoying yourself and thinking and letting life flow on have always belonged to the Mediterranean culture.

AG It's different in the north. It's a struggle. I remember how we used to go and look at the waves when I was a child. It's as though something was moving on your behalf. And there's a strength there that also invites you to think, but in much more 'aggressive' terms. To an extent, I associate the Basque character with that. It's a character of struggle, of challenge, of strength. However, the Mediterranean character is something else. It's lax, and yes, it's hedonistic. I always say that what I like about Madrid is Las Vistillas, because you can see the Casa de Campo and it's like seeing the sea. That's the moment when I relax. When you live beside the sea, you have a relaxed vision that allows you to think differently and tranquilly. That must influence the way you behave. The Mediterranean—specifically in Barcelona—has taught me what they call sensibility, and also something of the taste for hedonism, that pleasure in observing things that are made simply to look pretty.

(TEACHING)

RÚ Let's get back to reality. Do you somehow transmit all that knowledge and skill you've built up?

AG I give masterclasses from time to time. In them, I set about dismantling myself, because that's what you have to do. When I say I have lots of doubts in my work, people begin to empathise. I say to them, 'Sometimes I don't know where to begin'. But it's true, because I also have many limitations.

RE You can turn what might seem a disadvantage into your ally. That was said by another architect, Frank Lloyd Wright: the good architect turns his problems into his allies.

AG And also knowing how to turn round and renounce some of your ideas. That was a lesson Bigas Luna taught me. I remember we were making *Golden Balls* in Benidorm, and we had a fabulous idea. Production came along and told us it couldn't be done, to which Bigas calmly replied, 'Well, we'll do something else. Something better will come up'. That shows confidence, and it's more practical than wasting your time fighting over something.

RÚ An *idée* should never be *fixe*.

SKILL

RE One has a way of doing things, but it changes with the initial variables. It's no use being obsessed with something. It's more important to recognise the value of what you come across. I always give the example of Fleming with penicillin. You have to be prepared and to know how to see in order to discover things, and to find something even when you're investigating something else. Keynes also said, 'When reality changes, I too consider changing my ideas if necessary'. Doubt is part of our work, and learning is part of the profession.

AG That ability to renounce things that might seem fantastic to us in our work and replace them with others, without stubborn insistence, is something I always recommend to students, since if something can't be done, something else will occur to you. It doesn't matter. I work like that.

RE Going on to learn how to see. Things aren't linear. I always say the creative process isn't linear, although we narrate it in a linear fashion.

RÚ How often do you finish a design in the same way you started it?

RE Very seldom. In fact, in our field, the industry imposes lots of directives and conditions. They often say to you, 'No, this has to be done this way'. And that's fine, because limitations make the object acquire a greater formal coherence which you wouldn't have achieved on your own. You have to solve problems, not create problems that are already solved. That's the difference.

(ADAPTABILITY)

AG That ability to adapt you're talking about is perfect.

RE You have to know the laws that govern creative processes. Someone told me that there's lyric, epic and narrative in them. First comes the part involving fantasy; then the epic, which is the construction; and afterwards the narrative, when you can now tell the story. And it's not linear. It's never linear. Projects begin and sometimes reach points that are out on a limb, but you find yourself working with a thread that allows you to stitch it all together.

AG It's rather as Picasso said: 'May inspiration catch you while you're working.' You have to be on the spot.

RE And you have to know how to see when an idea appears. Or to put it another way, when the ideas come, to know how to see them.

AG Which is turning the negative into something good, or making a value out of what appears to be a difficulty.

RE That ability to turn it around makes it more interesting, because if not, you end up repeating yourself. There's a problem of inbreeding in creative sectors, because we all start from the same sources. Transversality is very interesting. I come from architecture, and I transmit my vision and experience to design, and vice versa. In fact, I sometimes advise my clients on the choice of furnishings. Putting myself in the user's place helps me when I have to come up with a new design.

AG Do you know an architect friend of mine from Barcelona called Barba Corsini?

RÚ The one who did the apartments of La Pedrera?

AG His son. Well, he said to me one day, 'When I'm commissioned to design a house, the first thing I do is go to the place and sleep there.' It's not just seeing the plot of land. You have to see where the sun comes up, where it goes down…

RE Returning to the object, that happened to me when I started to design. I found it tremendously hard to design furnishings without thinking they were for some particular place. Seeing the person, the place and the surroundings gives you a great many parameters.

AG Because if not, it's all too abstract.

RE All the more if you're doing a film set and you have to design pieces you need which are for that setting alone.

AG For *The Skin I Live In*. we designed a carpet of eleven metres by five and a half that they made for us in Crevillent. And we made some extensions for the chairs to give them what we thought would be the optimum size for them to function visually. Someone else might come along and not realise that, but it seems to you that it can't be any other way.

RE People either realise or don't realise, but the things are there.

AG I always say that if I don't believe it, I can't do it. I have to agree with what I'm doing.

RE Subjective perception, which is always there. Even the profane person with no understanding sees it in some way. They can't explain it, but they perceive it.

AG They may not verbalise it, but they can perceive it.

(SUSTAINABILITY)

RÚ It's almost better not to touch on the subject of sustainability, because if you throw away everything you construct…

AG We throw it all away. It's a disaster. Mind you, we also recycle quite a lot. It depends on the construction system that's being used. In Madrid, things are often constructed in a way that functions like a Meccano set. There are some panels that measure three by one, and when you design, you're already thinking in terms of that module. A three-metre-high wall, for example. Afterwards, the whole thing is papered over on both sides with Kraft paper and glued from top to bottom. Finally, it's painted and tensed like a drum. The wall looks perfect. When it's dismantled, it's kept and used again.

RÚ Is it always done that way in your sector?

AG No. I find what my French colleagues are doing very interesting, for example, because they approach construction in a different way. Here, you nearly always hire a firm that already has its *modus operandi*. In other countries, a construction team is always formed for each project, and they prioritise a construction system that will allow maximum recycling.

In France, the government provides financial aid so that nearly all the used material can be kept in industrial warehouses and processed so that it can be used again for future projects. Everything is controlled through the union of art department workers, who also try, for instance, not to use products with synthetic dissolvents, especially for paint. It's an initiative that's still in its early phase, but it's very necessary. Here, for the time being, we're at the back of the line.

RE In this matter, there's nothing for it but to make the whole system sustainable. I mean it has to be turned into a culture that eventually gives rise to a standard. Moreover, there has to be legislation so as to leave no other option. We're currently at a moment when not all the variables have been given parameters, and it's very easy just to use the label of sustainability as a marketing strategy.

AG When I was small, I remember, recycling didn't exist because it was done automatically. In other words, nothing was thrown away. Everything was reused.

RE And food wasn't thrown away. In fact, many popular recipes come from taking advantage of leftovers. It's complicated, though. There are issues, like single-use packaging, that are very complicated to resolve. PET can be recycled, but people throw it on the ground. Collective awareness is extremely important. In my experience of mountain biking, even forest paths and trails are full of bottles and cans.

AG I go round picking them all up.

RÚ As you do with old furniture. Your warehouse is like entering Ali Baba's cave.

AG Right now, I have a storage space in Barcelona and another in the cellar of my house in El Ampurdán. The furnishings are designs from the sixties and seventies, with some from the eighties and a few art deco pieces. I've got a good collection, if the truth be told, especially of lamps. I took advantage of the pandemic to count them. I'm currently on about 1,000 or 1,150, more or less. But it's not ordinary collecting. In my case, it's a disease that comes in useful for my work. Just now, for example, we're making a replica of a Belgian wallpaper I have from the twenties, which we're going to use on a film set.

RE If you could mount an exhibition with all those objects, it would be like a giant stage setting.

AG Alfaro Hofmann does have it well set up. The building that houses his collection is tremendous. We once gave a talk together, and it was quite obvious that we came from two different worlds. He's all functional, all clean, and I'm just the opposite, all wow! I can put on an apron I like next to a lamp by Vico Magistretti. For me, that kind of mixture is fun. What's more, I like to invent false scenarios: 'That wallpaper with that ashtray beside that table…'

RE The interesting thing is that you can make a space plausible with just a few objects. With me, it's the other way round. I talk to the object from architecture, and you talk to space from the object.

STYLE

In the world of design, labels are inevitable. The best style is coherence, and a good design, essentially, must always be functional. The best of all are those that still have value after transcending their functionality. The same is true of architecture.

TACHY MORA (TM) + RAMÓN ESTEVE (RE)

TM I'm of the opinion that not all architects have the ability to design furniture.

RE I totally agree. But most architects think they do.

RÚ Not most of them. All of them, I'd say.

TM Perhaps you can explain to us what an architect has to do to be able to work well on a small scale.

RE I think it's as difficult to design a good chair as a good skyscraper. There are as many good skyscrapers as there are good chairs. Technically it's different, but conceptually it's the same. The establishment of parameters, the resolution and the way of confronting an object are not the same as with a building, but the conceptualisation can be similar. That is, a furnishing philosophy can spring from an architectural philosophy, but the two things are resolved in completely different ways. One question that must be taken into account is that contemporary design was born with the twentieth-century avant-garde architects, among other things because the schools of industrial design didn't appear until the sixties. It's a fact.

RÚ When you were studying, was design taught at the school?

RE One of the advantages I've had, coming from a training as an architect, is that I started to interest myself in design and work on it at a moment when it was regarded as a completely separate field from the world of architecture, as was interior decorating.

RÚ But did anyone talk about it?

RE I studied in Madrid and later taught in Valencia, and I never met anyone who spoke about it. I started designing at the same time as I started working on architectural projects, and that was the origin of my passion for the object, for the idea of generating atmospheres, environments and experiences that couldn't be expressed with words. The idea was to design a whole universe in each project.

RÚ It's very curious that all architects should think they're magnificent designers, because nobody taught you anything about design at architecture school. I don't know if it's still that way.

TM On the degree course in architecture, you can choose subjects oriented towards furniture design, or afterwards you can do a Master's.

RÚ That must be very recent.

RE Those degrees are very recent. There were no specific degrees related to those two disciplines until a very short time ago. In Valencia, I've had offers to direct Master's degrees. Although I find it very interesting, and I've had the opportunity to take part in some, I don't have the time for it right now.

TM Well, it would be a great help for the new generations.

RÚ Architects have no training at all as designers.

RE That's what happened to me. I started designing out of necessity, and I later turned it into a profession. I wasn't trained as a furniture designer, but I've always been fascinated by design. I was self-taught, something very common in the artistic world. In the schools, they give you an academic basis, but where you then take it is your own affair.

TM That happens in every profession.

RE In nearly all, but more in ours. They're such broad disciplines that the schools can only teach you the basics. They can't teach everything in five years. They can only provide the tools so that you can then go on learning and developing. Depending on where you focus your energy and your interest, you'll manage to create something of value with those tools. In my case, owing to a mixture of interest and chance, I've ended up designing furnishings to be produced industrially.

RÚ That would be the right focus. How many architects in Spain are currently designing commercial furnishings? I'd have to rack my brains to think of one. Usually, if they're planning an auditorium, they want to do the seating, or if they design a public space, they want to design the benches too. But they can't see much further than their own navel, and the manufacturers, who play along with them to get their commissions, end up ploughing their resources and technical capacity into it, neglecting all the rest. Some firms have gone under because of that.

TM Exactly. It fascinates me that most architects say with total conviction that they're fully equipped to design furnishings. One thing is designing furniture or equipment *ad hoc* for a particular space, and another is doing industrial design.

(MINIMALISM)

RÚ A lack of professional experience tends to lead to simplification, like a poorly understood minimalism.

RE Talking of minimalism, I very much like the author of *Pasado a limpio*, Josep Quetglas. It makes for very interesting reading. I don't know him personally, and I never had the opportunity to have him as a teacher, but I've read several of his books, and I like them very much. Quetglas talks about what minimalism is and how it cannot be extrapolated to architecture. The question is that minimalism in art means one thing, and when applied to architecture or design, it turns out to mean another. In art, it could be associated with that movement there was in the fifties and sixties, with Donald Judd, Sol LeWitt and so on.

RÚ In architecture, it would lead us to 'less is more'.

RE Minimalism in architecture is basically a movement where the pieces are a geometry with no symbolism and no reference to anything other than themselves. What they do, then, is to attach value to the environment. A minimalist piece in music would be, for example, the work *4'33''* by John Cage. What he does in this piece is to open a piano on a stage and sit there for four minutes and thirty-three seconds without playing it. In this way, the concert consists of the sound of a concert that is never heard. That atmosphere of silence is what he performs and records at that moment.

RÚ The great thing about it is that it can be done with any instrument, even a whole orchestra. When he premiered it in 1952, I believe the paying audience was less than amused.

TM You can't please everyone, otherwise it wouldn't be art.

RE And so minimalism in itself, without philosophising, has to do with an object so disconnected from meaning that it enhances the value of what is around it, like a prism by Donald Judd or Dan Flavin's fluorescents. It's true that the structures of Sol LeWitt bear a relation to my first collection of furniture, Na Xemena. They're pieces that derive from an essential geometry, which to an extent is what I was exploring at that time. There may be a connection there, even if mainly formal, with pure and essential minimalism as an artistic movement. In architecture and design, that lack of meaning or enhancement of the value of the surroundings are not objectives in themselves. Minimalism might be understood as a movement that seeks a certain essentialism.

TM Do you feel comfortable when it's said your work is minimalist? Do you think it might just as easily be connected in your case with the austerity of Mediterranean architecture and interiors?

RE At some points, minimalism has been interpreted as a mere simplification of reality, but that's a mistake. It's not a question of removing elements so that it will seem essential, but of condensing them without eliminating parameters. I believe in not renouncing anything but in manifesting and materialising it with the minimum, so that what remains, the result, the essence, will acquire much greater value and clarity, and so that the principal is not distorted by the accessory or blurred by the anecdotal. In both design and architecture, that emphasis on the resolution of detail is not a hankering after preciosity but a way to make the initial concept gain strength and transmit itself in all its intensity.

TM Then how do you go about getting yourself linked to minimalism?

RE No, I don't go about anything of the kind. In some way, I appear as such in certain publications. They label me. The first time it happened was when I designed the Na Xemena house. When I had to give an account of that project, I took the structures of Sol LeWitt as a referent, but not as the starting point of the project, merely as a reference for explaining it.

RÚ You don't identify with that label.

RE In fact, a lot of contemporary architecture is driven by an urge to be structural and display itself naked. 'Less is more' meant a search for maximum intensity with minimum elements. I prefer to talk about concretion and condensation.

RÚ An interesting concept.

RE Another thing that interests me and has to do with style is that I don't try to force my identity onto the product. There's design with a capital 'D', which is cultured design, and on the other hand there's anonymous design, which comes from a tradition and a culture that's generated objects. I like creating an *auteur* design, but I want it to have the universal or essential nature of an object that wasn't the work of a designer, but which belongs to a culture and provides a simple solution for a need. In a way, that's what is illustrated by the book by Jasper Morrison that we've occasionally discussed. But I discovered it long before.

RÚ You're referring to *Super Normal*, which he wrote with Naoto Fukasawa.

RE I've been aware of the idea behind that book for more than twenty years, and I don't think it had even been written then. I've always been interested by anonymous architecture. In a way, Na Xemena inherits the spirit of the Mediterranean architecture of Ibiza, but at the same time it's a contemporary architecture with cultured references to the architecture of the twenty-first century. That happens in most of my designs. Right now, I'm thinking of the Casilda collection and many other pieces that are the way they are because that's how they have to be. They're designed by an author, but in my opinion they aspire to the austerity, freshness and humility of anonymity.

TM That's where I was trying to get to. When I asked you before if there might be some kind of connection between the Mediterranean style and minimalism, this is what I meant. I wasn't thinking so much of Na Xemena and that clear nexus you've just explained: that collection of furnishings made for this house, which is like a contemporary reinterpretation of the traditional Mediterranean dwelling. But it's true that in the Mediterranean tradition, in its style of building and living, there's an austerity and a simplicity, though with maximum functionality, that connects closely with what we were talking about before.

RE In traditional architecture, that essence comes from the scarcity of resources. That's shown perfectly by Bernard Rudofsky's fantastic book entitled *Architecture without Architects*. When you have only enough energy and resources for minimum solutions, you're almost forced to do something essential and purified. That's interesting, because now we do it from a conceptual point of view or as a reaction to the excesses of a society that can afford greater luxuries. However, we still look for objects that will draw us towards that purity, which also has to do with the spiritual desire for everything to be much more essential.

In particular, some of the solutions and objects of the Mediterranean tradition you're talking about are related to that absence of means or resources, because at certain periods of history, whether we're talking about Rome, Greece or, as in this case, the peasants of Ibiza, we find highly impoverished cultures that have lived with an architecture and a set of structures that barely rise above subsistence level. It's then that some marvellous objects are created, because that austerity is turned in the end into magnificent artistic codes. And yes, it's true there's a proximity and a parallelism between the architecture of this humble Mediterranean and that essential architecture or design which might at some point have been called minimalism.

TM Yes, but the style is not the same across the whole Mediterranean basin. On the islands, owing to a lack of resources and evident logistical questions, the austerity is more pronounced.

RE The style on the Iberian mainland is austere too, if you're talking about popular architecture.

RÚ In other parts of the Mediterranean basin, such as Morocco, they're not so minimalist.

TM Absolutely. What I'm trying to find out is whether your tendency towards minimalism might have come to you as an inheritance from the Mediterranean architectural and ornamental style of your surroundings, which is often austere. In the pottery of Talavera de la Reina, there isn't so much minimalism…

RE That's true. They're also different periods and social structures. A lot of the architecture and objects you're talking about originate in the countryside and are found in totally different societies. A society on the mainland has nothing to do with one on an island. Islanders have always been much poorer. In fact, their economic development started four minutes ago.

RÚ Four minutes that are actually four decades.

(DECORATION)

TM Since we're talking about ornament, I'd like to change the subject a little bit and talk about decorating, which can be another thorny subject. Do you feel comfortable or uncomfortable with the word?

RE Some words are regarded with contempt, as the word 'design' sometimes is too. When a word is used a great deal, it immediately tends to sound hollow. Sometimes, from so much use, it's robbed of its essential sense or meaning. In the case of decorating, I think we're at a time when a lot of things are under review. In particular, I'm someone with a natural tendency towards the essential, and I surround myself with very few objects. That's what my houses are like: they're full of what's necessary, and I give away what I don't need. I get rid of it somehow.

TM For you, then, what is décor? How do you understand it?

RE I always try to make sure that with the essential things, meaning the architecture itself, its volumes and the arrangement of its elements, nothing else is necessary to make a space inhabitable. However, I understand that we need to construct our habitat with objects that have to do with the memory of our lives, objects that say what we are like. But that's not something I contribute. It's completed by the person who inhabits the place in order to consolidate their identification with it.

TM Things that connect us with life.

RE I have an austerity that's almost monastic. As a friend said to me some time ago: 'When I want a Cistercian cell, I'll call you.' And I feel very comfortable in mediaeval monasteries, with their stone walls concentrating all the work and the texture. But I understand that people should want more things that connect with their lives. It's something we find in the Eames' Case Study House 8.

RÚ Decorating is dressing a space.

RE Because spaces don't always have the ability to solve everything for themselves. When that doesn't happen, which is 99% of the time, you can use facing, lighting and objects to give any space quality, value and personality. We're talking about a space open to the public, like a restaurant, for example, which tells you about the chef's gastronomic philosophy.

RÚ In a house, the space tells you what the person living there is like.

RE We're at a moment when décor or interior design have become extremely important. When I design a project from zero, I'm thinking about the interior decorating from the very start. It's implicit. Nevertheless, when we're dealing with a place that's already constructed, we plan only the interior. I've designed restaurants in anodyne spaces, and I've had to resort to placing objects that would tell a story and have a narrative. That's decorating, and it's not auxiliary. It's necessary to construct the space.

TM What kind of objects do you keep?

RE Very few. I have furniture from the forties and fifties, like the Torres Clavé chair, the BKF or the Gandula Barceloneta, and also pieces by Milá and Moragas. I very much like collecting pieces by the first Spanish designers, and I would in this case like to build up a collection of valuable pieces that fall under that heading. That's where furniture is concerned. As for other utensils, I try to make sure they're as pretty as possible and bear a relation to the place where I'm going to use them.

RÚ No art?

RE People criticise me for not having a single picture, even though I'm an art lover.

TM I get criticised for that as well.

RE When I travel, I go and look at art, but I don't have a single piece at home. I've been given a few works, and I have them hidden away in cupboards.

TM That's not right.

RE I admit it's a little excessive.

TM I'm rather the same. I often wonder if it's a style of life or a style of person. In my case, it's the first, probably because I've moved house twenty-four times. I've always had very few things because of that, so as to be able to move around easily.

RE That's very interesting.

TM When I was young, everything I had used to fit in the car. Sometimes, I even had space left over.

RE I greatly like the way Marcel Duchamp saw things. He didn't want an attachment to any object, and when he moved house, he left it all behind. It was like starting a new life somewhere else. That's the concept of 'not dragging your past behind you'. I drag few memories with me, so I'm not much of a fetishist. I don't have photos anywhere, which is a little extreme. The thing is, though, that I like to project my life onto an empty page, and I'm quite happy that way. When my friend made that remark about the Cistercian cell, he was trying to bother me, but I took it as a compliment and made it my own.

TM And yet I can fall desperately in love with an object, as if it were a person. And the day it breaks for whatever reason, by accident or because it's got old, it makes me so sad that I start to cry.

RE You're saying something interesting about where we connect. You have few things, but those you do own have an enormous affective value.

TM Affective or aesthetic.

RE In both our cases, I think, there's no room for anything that's not aesthetic. What I do like having is books. It's true that I keep moving them around and filling up bookcases.

TM Every so often, I give mine away. That way, they can be consulted and enjoyed by others. I only keep the really important ones.

RE Do you? I don't. If someone asks me for a book, I prefer to give them a new one. If it's still in print, I buy it again, because I know I'm not going to get it back. I think that one day I'm going to need it for something—a talk, writing an article, whatever. There are some books I don't like to let go of because it's as though part of my learning were being taken away from me.

(HONESTY)

TM What else shall we talk about?

RÚ About ethics, about honesty, which is something that's not often discussed in our sector. When a project gets shelved, which I imagine must happen to a few, do you try to palm it off on someone else?

TM I love that question.

RE There are designers who work that way, going around with a book of products. It's not the way I proceed. I try to come up with an exclusive proposal for each brand. Normally, in fact, we always have to start with a briefing, except when the brand is one we work with quite regularly, when we're the ones to propose new directions to them. A final design is not exactly the same as the initial idea, because when you start to work with a brand, there's an evolution, the industrial process optimises the proposal, and in the end something better always comes out.

At heart, there's an ethical vision in contemporary design and architecture in the sense of designing honestly, looking for a link between the concept and production of an element. Both in a building and in an object, there's a concern that form, use and manufacture should somehow go in the same direction. This coherence is something that's almost come down to us from Giedion and his essays *The Eternal Present: The Beginnings of Art and Architecture*, where he specifies the constants in the art world since the origins of humanity.

RÚ It was like that in the most essential periods of history, and ceased to be like that in those which are not so essential.

RE And that doesn't mean that some periods are more interesting than others. For example, the Baroque is greatly reviled, and yet I find some of its manifestations extremely interesting. It's the least essential period, if we leave aside its ornamentation. Among other things, because of its spatial structure, the treatment of light, and the new concept of the urban space as an architectural space. It's the great moment of theatre and stage design. We're now living in a Baroque period.

RÚ Do you think so?

RE Absolutely.

TM We live in an eclectic period, I'd say.

RE But within that eclecticism, we're living in a period of theatre and stage design. We're living at a moment that consists of spectacle fortified by the digital world.

TM That's true. On the question of ethics, and picking up on what you said before about honesty, there was a lot of talk some years ago about honest design. I'd say it was something that even became fashionable. I think it emerged around the time of *Super Normal*…

RÚ Until it got a bit tiresome. It's fine for things to be 'super normal', but you also have to evolve a little bit.

TM Of course, that's where I'm heading. What is honesty in design, then?

RE What's happened is that after minimalism, the theatricality I'm talking about has arrived. I think we've gone through some years of superessentialism, and then there came a time when tendencies pointed towards that theatricality, although now it's fortunately coming to an end. In my case, it has to do with that ethic of 'less is more'. But I repeat that this is a more personal vision.

TM That would mean being honest with yourself, with the way you design.

RE You do what you think you must, not what circumstances dictate.

TM Or trends.

RE That's right. I think I've generally remained quite firm in that sense.

RÚ Being honest is going against the grain, isn't it?

RE Yes, exactly. But the grain can also come looking for you. Or it finds you on your way back. Obviously, no-one can stand completely apart. The grain influences you in some way, but one thing is being slightly influenced and another is completely losing your course. Being dragged along a little by the current is very different from floating adrift.

RÚ Analysing trends as you do, what do you think is an honest design and a dishonest design? Could you give any examples?

TM One thing is being honest as a professional, and another that a design should be honest in itself. For me, in terms of industrial design, an honest design, to start with, is one that is fully functional. In that sense I'm very radical. A design must be perfectly conceived and produced to fulfil its function, it must be better than its predecessors, and it must be sustainable. Honesty has various parameters depending on the type of product. Then there are the aesthetic aspects, which are more subjective. An honest design can be many things, but the most important is that it should fulfil its function. For me, a design that doesn't function well is not honest. I'm still talking in terms of industrial design.

RÚ Rather than dishonest, it would be badly designed.

TM Of course, but these things get put on the market… Sometimes there are things which are not badly designed but badly produced.

RE Quite honestly, I couldn't tell you what an honest design is. The functionality of an object is its starting point. An object is born of a function—it happens with architecture too—but there are objects which transcend functionality, and when they cease to have that function, they still have value. That, for me, is an object with a good design. Not only is it well resolved, but when it is no longer used, it remains valuable and attractive. I think honesty is related more to what you've said, and to your way of doing things. If you're able to generate a language or a way of designing or of seeing life, and of encapsulating it in the objects you design, that ethics and that honesty may well form part of it.

RÚ I'd like to talk about honesty in a different sphere, and to step in a puddle we often come across in this profession, which is the question of copies or 'inspirations'. Have you been copied?

RE Yes, of course. A lot. Right now, they're copying the entire Vondom catalogue in China, and I don't know where else, using even the photos and everything.

RÚ Have you ever been accused of being a copycat?

RE Never. And I've been doing things for more than twenty-five years. It may be that among the proposals that arise when you're working with a large team, there's something that looks a lot like something else. It's sometimes happened to me, because you don't know the whole market. But when I've detected some similarity, I've automatically discarded that way forward. My designs are always born of an idea, a concept or a simple detail. A chair can be born from a mitre joint, but it doesn't come from saying: 'I've seen such-and-such a chair and let's see what I can do that might approximate it.' Maybe that's where honesty comes into design.

RÚ There are people who are very clever at being dishonest.

RE What a lot of people are doing is exactly that, taking something successful and approximating it. It happens with Posidonia. There are a thousand pieces of furniture approximating it. Fortunately, that design is so well balanced that when someone approximates it very closely, it resembles it too much, and when they don't, it has no charm.

RÚ Success is not so easy to copy.

RE Because many of my pieces have been successful because of their normality, which enshrines a value that we haven't talked about, and which is one of the cornerstones of design: proportion. When you work with such essential forms, the proportions are the most important thing of all. That balance between the parts is very difficult to achieve, and it's the basis of beauty. When you endow the piece with that harmony, the copy breaks it. And that's the difficulty of copying.

TM Do you design the things you want to?

RE In most cases, yes.

TM And then you go off in search of a firm to produce it? How do you do it?

RE I begin by talking to them, as when I make a house for a client. I'm designing a made-to-measure suit, but it's my suit. That is, both the client and myself have to identify with each other. It's the same with design. The design has to be both the brand's and my own.

TM In other words, a bit of yourself and a bit of the brand.

RE When a brand has a very strong identity, it makes it more comfortable in a certain way, because part of the process has already been done for you, and you try to make its values your own. But the brand also wants something from you. Once more, it's a question of balance.

CULTURE

The type of firm you design for ends up marking the direction you take. It can be a manufacturer, which has its own factory, or it can be what in Spain is called an 'editor', a company without a factory that outsources its 'editions' to the supplier required for each project. There are parallels with the world of culture.

ALBERTO ANAUT (AA) + RAMÓN ESTEVE (RE)

RÚ Every time I say that a firm is a 'design editor', my book publishing friends tell me off.

AA It's a suitable term.

RÚ When BD Ediciones de Diseño appeared in 1972, it was the first furniture editor in Spain. What was the difference? That BD didn't have a factory, as was usual then. At La Fábrica, I don't think you had a printing press to produce your books, either.

AA No. That would have been all we needed.

RÚ So if you work for a particular manufacturer that uses specific technology, you have to adapt to it. If you work for an editor, the field is theoretically open for you to work with other things.

RE We work for both. It's good to work with a manufacturer, because I find it easier to design something if I know the manufacturing processes. I see the limitations and discover possibilities, and the combination of the two helps me create pieces that go with those processes, not against them.

We also work with editors because the world of design, when all is said and done, is also a philosophy, a lifestyle. They're very hackneyed words, but it's true. A brand is a way of seeing the world. A good brand gives you a product which fits into a collective that sees the world in a similar way or is excited by the same things. There's a language, there's a series of codes implicit in the piece that connect with a group of people.

RÚ Vondom is a brand-cum-manufacturer, or vice versa.

RE And I think it sometimes conditions you positively to use a particular technology. Working with MDF, which doesn't have a factory and is more of an editor that works with almost anything, can be more difficult. Especially when they tell you they want an iconic piece. What are you supposed to do then?

AA An iconic piece is achieved with time, isn't it? It has to become iconic.

RE When you start out, you almost know already. I've argued for this many times. When I've been quite sure that a piece was going to work, I've insisted with my customary vehemence that it should go ahead. I've very seldom been wrong.

AA And do you see that from the very first drawing?

RE I think so. In the studio, when we say, 'This piece is going to catch on', it usually does and it sells. Please don't misinterpret me. I don't wish to be presumptuous, but it's true that it's happened to me with certain collections. On one occasion, I remember insisting for two years that it should go on the market, and when it did, it was a success.

RÚ Alberto, are you able to look at a book, or an issue of *Matador* or something, and say, 'This is going to be a smash'?

AA In the book world, it's complicated. A publisher with a lot of experience, who's now nearly retired from the market, said to me one day, 'Look, Alberto, there are four types of book: the ones you like, you think will succeed, and do succeed, which are the only good ones; the ones you think will succeed and you like, but don't succeed, which is the majority; the ones you don't like and you put out only because you think they'll succeed and then don't succeed, which are the ones that most annoy you because you knew you shouldn't have done them; and the ones you don't like, you think are not going to succeed, and finally do succeed, which are the surprises'.

RE You've described exactly what happens with furniture.

AA Yes, but I think there's a clearer market for design than for books.

RE Because a book has to be read, whereas you can fall in love with a design at first sight.

AA Which kind of piece do you most enjoy designing?

RE A chair is always a challenge. Its parameters are so few that it's very hard to do something that stands out and makes an impact.

AA It's difficult to make it original.

RE To give it an identity, to make it recognisable, and to ensure it's not a plagiarised version of something else is very difficult.

RÚ The same is true of architecture.

RE One of the differences is that in design, pieces are almost intuitive. If you have a bright idea, even if it then proves difficult to resolve it, you know that's what's going to be left at the end. In architecture, however, the processes are so long that the project can evolve, and the idea you started out with can end up turning into another.

(HISTORY)

AA In your opinion, what characteristic differences are there between a design made by an architect and a design by someone directly dedicated to furnishing?

RE That it's born directly from an architectural context, either from the line of work the architect is pursuing at that moment, or from a specific building. My thesis, *La fabricación del interior*, which I later turned into a blog, is about this. What I did was to study the relationship between furnishings and architecture in the twentieth-century avant-gardes. It turns out that nearly all the great designs of the century were made by architects, and I say this without being corporatist.

RÚ It's the consequence of a need. I'm sure that you too have looked for something you didn't find on the market and ended up planning it yourself. In the twentieth century, that happened to everybody. They approached furniture design from the conviction that it is necessary for furnishings to be developed coherently with the space that houses them if the architecture is to yield all its sensory potential. Those words are yours. In your thesis, you tried to show the relationship between furniture and architecture, and how the first acts as a link between a place and the person who lives in it, amplifying the perception of the experience of inhabiting it.

RE But it's not a dogma. An architect can be mistaken in trying to transfer the architecture to the furnishings when it cannot be done directly. Furniture has its requirements. It has to be light, comfortable, ergonomic…

AA What an architect tries to do is sometimes too recherché.

RE Quite so. There came a moment when the avant-garde architects discovered the importance of furnishings. When Le Corbusier did the pavilion for L'Esprit Nouveau in 1925, he equipped it with a chair designed by Thonet. When you see it now, there's something that doesn't fit in, and it's because the architecture is more advanced than the furniture design.

RÚ By then he was already collaborating with Charlotte Perriand.

RE Four years later, they started to work together on the LC collections, which appeared at the Salon d'Automne in 1929. Here, it is now possible to perceive a harmony between container and content, and to see how the scale of the object and that of the space enhance each other mutually to create an augmented experience. That doesn't mean that all projects must have their specific furnishings. Such a task couldn't be assumed. Designing furniture is not the same as designing architecture. The parameters are very different, and every piece of furniture is a project. Even if the conceptualisation is the same, the requirements and the resolution are not.

AA It's a stricter programme, isn't it?

RE Of course. Mies van der Rohe made furniture for his houses too, but he put it in when he could. There are some very interesting stories about that, like the one about the Villa Tugendhat, whose owners found it with Mies's furniture in it without having requested it, and who liked it when they saw it and decided to leave it.

AA But when you design a piece of furniture for a particular space and you end up marketing it separately for any other space, it gets decoupled.

RE Not necessarily. A space can be furnished with pieces that harmonise with it even though they weren't designed for that project. Le Corbusier and Mies ended up doing that because they were forced to, as today's market offerings didn't exist at the time of the first avant-garde movements. There's such a wide availability of furnishings now that designing is unnecessary. It's more because you feel it ought to be that way than out of necessity.

AA The contemporary architect has become a little bit like a Renaissance man, or the man who thinks of everything. I don't know if, for example, you'd also like to choose the art that will be displayed in those spaces.

RE I've intervened when the occasion has arisen. I'm passionate about contemporary art. I'm not a specialist, but it's a fundamental complement to architecture. In fact, there's nothing like a good project with good artworks. Works of art are not mere objects that drop into a space. A good arrangement establishes a dialogue with the space that contains them, heightens or contrasts with their setting or integrates with its scale, and plays with light and perspective.

AA I sometimes get the feeling that this Renaissance vision clashes with the living conditions that houses demand from people, or with the working conditions in offices. With the changes of the last few years, like teleworking and so forth, I imagine everything has to be thought out differently. But when you look closely at a piece of furniture, like a chair, you see it has to fulfil functions closely related to use and comfort. Owing to the way we live, we don't make the most of our houses and workspaces because the right products haven't always been created. Don't you think so?

RE Regarding that Renaissance vision you were talking about, there's something I haven't mentioned yet because it didn't appear in the twentieth century but in the nineteenth. This is the *Gesamtkunstwerk*, that idea of the 'total work of art' which came from the Vienna Secession and then fell somewhat into disfavour. We need only recall Adolf Loos's essay 'Ornament and Crime', in which he criticised the ornamentation of useful objects because he preferred them not to be so thoroughly designed and to have a spontaneous component. The Bauhaus resumed this point of view, as such an ideology had its entire contemporary outlook behind it, and it naturally wanted to take it to its limits.

AA Then how is it that this intellectual, theoretical and, let's say, humanist position clashes with the living conditions we've actually created?

RE When the proposals have been good, they've worked well. For example, another master I like very much is Frank Lloyd Wright. In the thirties, he designed the Johnson Wax building and designed its tables, cupboards, chairs, lamps...

RÚ As many as 48 different models, manufactured by Steelcase.

RE All the office furnishings were produced with account duly taken of the ergonomics and the technology, which then consisted of the typewriter and the telephone. It's a magnificent space designed as a great working hall. The function was and remains the primary thing, but the good design transcends its utility. Do you mean something along those lines?

AA Yes, well... Because of our system of life, the market establishes certain conditions for collective projects—not so much for individual ones—that people perhaps feel uncomfortable living with, don't you think?

RE Now I don't understand you.

AA From the architectural point of view.

RE Give me an example.

AA Do we live in houses where it's possible to live well?

RE People need places to live in and occupy what is built. They adapt to the house, not the other way around. They occupy them, but they lack that emotional, cultural or spiritual part that comes from good architecture. The dwellings that are being built now respond to a socio-economic structural reality.

AA Which lays down some economic conditions for construction.

RE In which there's very little room for architecture. I make public architecture, on a larger scale, but I also make single-family dwellings, which require a lot of dedication and consume a great deal of energy.

AA It takes a very long time, doesn't it?

RÚ It's the *haute couture* of architecture.

RE I've tried to do a *prêt-à-porter* based on the experience of *haute couture*. The promoters want it, but they're not prepared to sacrifice profit in return for higher quality, even though it might mean an increase in added value and, in time, create a brand. And that doesn't happen in the design industry. They're much more receptive to that concept of a brand, a lifestyle, the segment and the client's philosophy.

AA In design, multiplication is also a factor of success.

RE Yes. In design, we work with royalties, which is a kind of adventure that involves sharing the success with the client. It's a formula I'm happy with. In fact, I'd like it to happen with architecture as well. If the project is successful, it should mean a deferred return. In the sector of industrialisation, which is now emerging, there might be room for such a model. Things are changing.

RÚ Because it's very practical. You save construction time, and the cost is a fixed price.

AA It also has a set of contemporary values. Sustainability, for example.

RE It has all the advantages of an industrial process, where there's much more control over all the procedures and a greater capacity for optimisation and regulation in terms of both energy consumption and the management of materials, waste and so on. In the end, you get more quality and better guarantees.

RÚ Besides that, it's getting more and more difficult to find a specialised work force for construction.

AA Craftsmanship is being lost, and finding someone who can lay a floor tile properly for you is a miracle.

RE The big promoters are starting to have serious problems with this. I do everything with firms which, even if they're very technological, work with artisans, who make things to measure, and I try to take them with me.

AA Just look at the word you use for a chap who lays bricks. Now he's an artisan. Watch out!

RE A bricklayer is an artisan, a blacksmith is an artisan and a carpenter is an artisan. There's an important difference between serial industrialisation and making things to measure, which is much more closely related to artisanal skills and crafts. These require a lot of training, which is sadly harder and harder to find these days.

(MODEL)

AA What's your studio like?

RE My studio is where I live. It's a house and studio combined. I found a plot of land in El Carmen, an emerging district between the IVAM and the Centre del Carme, and I put up a small building there that is a kind of manifesto of my life. It's linked to my work and to a surrounding area of historic and cultural value. In the last few years, we've grown a great deal and we've rented a space next to the studio, where we've put the design team. In that way, they manage themselves more independently without losing cohesion with the rest of the team.

AA How many people works with you?

RE At the moment, there are twenty-five to thirty of us.

AA This business of living where you work is something I saw with Patricia Urquiola. The system can have the drawback that you don't completely disconnect from work unless you really want to. On the other hand, it can be an advantage, because life in the end is very circular.

RE I don't want to disconnect.

AA There are no timetables any more. The pandemic did away with them. Now I get whatsapps at midnight. We're a bit nutty. Working timetables are now circular.

RÚ For some people, it's always been that way.

RE I've always lived like that. I've got my clients accustomed to not calling me at weekends. The same goes for the team. If I send someone a message on a Saturday, it's because it's vitally important.

AA You think it over first.

RE We agree on a code. If I have an idea one Saturday afternoon, what I do is send an email. When we send emails, it means it's not urgent. It's just so that we don't forget. When it's a whatsapp, it is urgent.

RÚ This profession has no timetables.

RE I want to slacken the pace. But with the amount of work we've been getting lately, I see I can't. Our professionals are vocational, and I want to carry on working until the end, as long as I can. For me, working is living.

AA Are you preparing your studio for that moment?

RE Yes, we started to prepare it a few years ago so that it would evolve towards an associative structure. Keeping up our activity is financially very difficult—you know from your own experience how complex it is. And you can find yourself at the end of the road with less strength and a series of obligations or commitments that won't let you carry on without abandoning your team. The idea is to plan a handover and form a group of associates who will gradually take over the reins. My idea is to evolve in that way, as many others have done, but on a small scale, because in the end everyone has their own scale.

AA Yes, but the model is viable.

RÚ As long as you know how to delegate.

AA Do you have a very personal way of working, or do you give your team opportunities?

RE We assigned the roles some time ago, and my post is that of creative director. Projects always have to start out from my concepts so as not to lose our identity. In the development, however, there's a lot the team can contribute.

AA What kind of people do you want in the studio? Do you work with young people?

RE In general, the studio is younger than I am. I'm the oldest in every way.

AA By young, I mean 23 years old.

RE At 23, they haven't qualified yet. The male and female directors—there are more women than men in the team—are around 40, and all the rest are around 30.

AA Does that youth give you inspiration?

RE That's a complicated question. I've fitted in with certain furniture producers or editors because I have a fairly sober, fairly serene and fairly timeless philosophy. Creating pieces that say something to you and are so apparently normal is really quite hard. It's much easier to differentiate yourself with something excessive. Young designers find it very difficult to start out in this profession and suddenly have to restrain themselves.

RÚ They get a dose of reality.

RE I think that when someone is studying at school, that's the moment to experiment and to stimulate creativity, and it's right not to set up so many barriers. That time will come. On the other hand, there are the publications which set trends, and which are not necessarily aligned with the reality of the market. In the line we're working in, there has to be that creativity and freshness, but it has to be restrained, and that's difficult.

AA So to reach that point, we might say that what's required is maturity.

RE It's very unusual for someone who's very young to propose a marvellous piece and for us to accept it just as it is. It is true, however, that a proposal can sometimes open up a valid path for us. It's interesting when young people put you in check, making you go where you normally wouldn't, and when you get the chance in the end to turn it into something solid. That works.

AA They propose a material, or they propose…

RE No, because they don't know that much about processes. I was an architecture teacher for many years, and I used to recommend repeatedly to my students that they should learn about processes to avoid becoming caretakers of catalogues and patents invented by others. Even if you use them later on, it's important to get to know them in depth and to question them so as to be able to come up with different results. It's the best way to avoid the inbreeding we suffer from so much in both architecture and design.

AA In other words, the profession is learned by working.

RE And visiting the professionals. The architect and the designer are like an orchestra conductor, who knows how to make use of the resources, which are the musicians, but has to know first how far a violin can go or how far a flute can go. It's necessary to know how much each can give of itself to be able to join it all together and produce something. There are products which are a single material and others which need different professional skills. Behind an armchair, there are carpenters, upholsterers, pattern designers…

RÚ And they have to be cherished.

RE Half of the ones who work with me are close associates. I'm even on friendly terms with some of them.

AA And what about your own team, the people you work with?

RE People from a lot of different countries have passed through the studio. They still come now, though the majority are from Spain. We like professionals from other countries to come because they always contribute a different vision.

RÚ And what about you at La Fábrica?

AA Well, our team is very varied. My partner and I have been friends since the age of six. We went to the same local primary school together. But later, when we started out 25 years ago, the world of cultural management didn't exist. It hadn't yet been developed. People came to us from the areas of history of art, communication or journalism. There were few close relationships, and although one person might end up bringing another, it wasn't like that from the start. I, for example, have made friends through work rather than working directly with friends, perhaps because it was a sector without a pool of professionals. Today, there's more going on in cultural management. We have a school, and we have a Master's degree course which is now taken by a lot of people. Even so, we like to work with professionals who are already trained. In other words, it suits us to work with people who don't start with us.

RE That's the reason why I have fewer foreigners than Spaniards. They don't have the same way of working because architecture and design are viewed differently. When I've taken on foreign personnel, specifically in architecture, they've had to go through a period of adaptation, because the management and focus of Spanish architecture are quite different from those of other countries. However, they've also helped us when it came to doing projects abroad, which is by no means easy. On the other hand, when my pupils have left to work abroad, things have gone very well for them. They've been able to join top studios, because the training in Spain up to now has been very good. Besides, I try to take on professionals with a bit of experience. Interns too, because of the commitments we have with the universities and the development of talent, but ours is not the type of studio based on internships. That doesn't work in our case because of the question of maturity we were commenting on earlier.

AA If you look after interns well, they can be very productive. Sometimes, though, they're not properly looked after. We've had people who have started to work with us, but over the first few years, they haven't really yielded that much. You see a person with talent, because that's obvious from the first moment, but it's only after a few years have gone by that someone starts to work well. When they've learned how to work, we might say.

RE It's the same with us. Exactly the same.

AA In the long run, in the professional arena, it's all very similar if you're in areas that have a creative component. Not everyone is good at everything, but the same things happen.

(EXCLUSIVITY)

RÚ In the world of design, a creator can work for a lot of different firms, but in the publishing world, it's more complex.

AA We're more jealous.

RÚ If you're a writer and you have a publisher, you've got to be faithful to them.

AA Publishing ventures are long-term, not for just one title. I think the same happens in design, though not so much. For instance, we publish Chema Madoz and Alberto García-Alix, and as publishers, we want to follow their entire careers. On the other hand, we publishers establish a style of book. It's true that the content is the author's, but the book is the publisher's. Otherwise, the market would get a little confused. I don't know if I'm explaining myself.

RE That happens with furniture too.

AA But you have more freedom to work with several others.

RÚ In the world of design, the *auteur* has that freedom. It's allowed, and it's not frowned upon. However, if you work for two firms that are competing, it's obviously a problem.

RE When they're from the same sector, someone's occasionally been bothered, even though we tread extremely carefully. We try to work with firms that are not in direct competition.

AA And also because it's seen more as the work of a studio. Photographers and writers are highly individual, and I think they're easier to 'hog', if I can put it that way, than when you're dealing with a studio. But anything can happen. I'm recalling the case of Rosa Montero, a successful writer who has a very peculiar system. She works with two publishers alternately, doing one book with one, the next with the other, and so on successively. Books that are totally compatible. She's managed to impose that system on her two publishers, and probably neither of them likes it, but neither wants to be the one that stops working with Rosa, who's an interesting, prestigious and popular author.

RÚ It's another way of remaining faithful. When designers become famous, they prefer spreading their love around.

AA In photography, I think we hog our artists more. I had an experience with one of the authors we habitually work with. He said to me, 'Taschen is trying to lure me. What shall I do?' Well, do a book with them. How am I going to tell him not to do a book with Taschen? In the event, it never came out. I came off wonderfully, and luckily for me, it didn't happen. But you have to be sensible. What's pointless is doing the same thing with different publishers.

RÚ These days, nobody's that sensible in the world of design. There are designers who shoot off in every direction and do very similar things for different clients.

RE That happens. And when you do that, you have to be very careful not to end up damaging your reputation, because you can't reinvent yourself every minute and do something completely different for a multitude of brands. It wouldn't even be coherent. You don't necessarily have to produce an easily recognisable line, but there must be a perceptible harmony and continuity when you put all the products together.

RÚ That formula of working for a lot of brands simultaneously only works if you're a firm, not an *auteur*. In branding, it's quite common. You hire the studio, as Alberto used to say.

AA Yes, but if the ideal client, the one you'd most like to have in the world, then came along and said to you, 'From now on, you work only for me and you make me one product a year', would you accept?

RE You couldn't maintain a studio with that, but for the moment, I have the capacity to produce much more.

RÚ And if, as a successful designer, the studio could maintain you?

RE On occasions I've tried to work for myself. It's always appealed to me to found my own brand, like Tom Dixon. That would be ideal for me, because you make no concessions. No matter how much affinity you have with a brand, there can always be differences, even if it's not a question of the product and is simply a matter of communication. Another model is that of Antonio Citterio, for whom B&B produces practically everything he designs. If a client came along and gave me *carte blanche* in every field, from the product to communication, I'd be happy to accept it.

AA But that also puts you in the client's hands, doesn't it?

RE Well, I'm imagining a hypothetical and ideal situation in which we'd have the same power to decide.

AA I'm remembering when we started with PHotoEspaña, which is a complex festival with dozens and dozens of participants, sponsors and everything. It was my first meeting of what we might call a financial rather than an artistic nature. There it was announced how much the festival would cost—I'm talking about twenty-five years ago—and I think it was about a hundred million pesetas. Then they said to me, 'Would you be willing to have it done by a single foundation?' They didn't say 'mine', but it was obvious. I was flabbergasted. I said to them, 'Give me twenty seconds to think about it'. And I said no.

No, because it wouldn't succeed. Because in that case, I was going to be in their hands, and besides, being under a single patronage would have prevented us from securing all the contributions we could have attracted. If you're going to impose your rubber stamp on a festival, it's going to cost five times more than it really does. It was the right decision to make. As an *auteur*, of course, it's different, but if you're your own producer, it's something else. Then you're one hundred per cent safe.

RE If my point of view were respected at every level in both the design and the communication strategy, then working for someone exclusively would be like having my own brand, and would even have the advantage of not having to worry about the financial management, the sales and the manufacturing. In that situation, I might have been comfortable. When you start to design, what you want is to develop your own creative universe. It's also true, as happened to you with that festival, that a series of synergies can arise. When I work with a lot of people, it indirectly teaches me things. I find it greatly enriching to work with different people.

AA And it gives you freedom. Because if someone suggests something unreasonable to you, you know that the solution is simply not to do it.

RE That's what happens to me with architecture, or with other clients. But I really would have liked to go into self-editing. I tried at one point, the project worked and the pieces did well, but it was killed off on the entrepreneurial side, which decided not to carry on, and I haven't had the energy to start another undertaking of that kind.

RÚ I'd say you might well fall into that temptation again.

RE Because you have greater control. What I like is the whole business of creative directing, not just designing the pieces. At Vondom, I've spent various periods as artistic director. Even with some other firms, like Talenti, I've given them a push at the start, making a catalogue and a stand for them so that they could gain consistency. It worked in both cases. In others, I've tried to propose similar things or collections that have been rejected, and I've had to take those proposals elsewhere, and listen to people's misgivings besides.

AA There's an expression which reflects that: it's like a dog in the manger.

RE Do you know what? Design is sometimes like strawberries, which go rotten. Even if a design is timeless, there's a time to release it. When you wait for a long time, you may regret it.

RÚ Because it's a sector where everything happens very fast.

RE And while a brand is thinking it over, another one brings out a product in a similar line. Then your design loses the force of novelty.

RÚ Creativity is worth nothing on its own. Among other things, the success of what you're designing has a lot to do with speed and opportunity.

RE Those two words are fundamental.

RÚ The public doesn't know that years can go by between a first sketch and what finally goes on the market. In that time, there may be other designers thinking of doing the same thing.

AA Yes, and what's more, all of them are starting from the same information.

RE It's curious that all the new things you see which surprise you were thought up at least two years earlier, and maybe even three or four. I'm not afraid of designing at speed, as Vondom allows me to. It's not an editor, it's an industry. It has machinery and a skilled technical team, and it's not afraid to take risks with a good design. With them, it's easier to stay fresh.

AA When we first put out the magazine *Matador*, one of my arguments was, 'I'm doing this because if I don't, I'm going to find it at the newsagent done by someone else. It won't be called *Matador*, but it'll be the same idea'.

RÚ And it'll be the last straw if the public likes it.

(CLIENT)

AA I'd like to look elsewhere and talk about the client. Not about your client, but about the manufacturer's final client. What are Spanish clients like?

RE In Spain, there's a culture of contemporary design. They were a minority at first, but a lot of things have happened, and now there's more culture and greater economic potential. There is a refined, cultured and well-travelled social class that is calling for design. There's also the influence of specialised publications, which have performed a fundamental task in spreading information. Nowadays, contemporary design has acquired a high social status, and on the other hand it has been democratised, becoming more accessible thanks to large low-cost brands. However, we're still a long way from Italy, France or the centre and north of Europe. In the Scandinavian countries, contemporary culture appears in every walk of life.

AA And don't you find that here?

RE We're on that path. There are very good Spanish brands and a very wide market.

RÚ People always talk about the eighties, but there was actually a huge production from the thirties up to that decade.

RE The Torres Clavé armchair dates from 1937. The GATEPAC, Bonet, Correa, Milá… and all the architects who designed furnishings. Carvajal made a fantastic armchair, Fisac has some magnificent pieces, and so does De la Sota…

AA We've had some extraordinary exhibitions at the Madrid Design Festival. At one of them, I remember, Rafael Moneo's daughter, Belén, who is also an architect, said, 'What an amazing impression! It's as though I were walking into the houses of my parents' friends'.

RÚ There was a time when people put that furniture in their houses, and it's worth wondering why that culture was lost in this country. In Milan, if you go into the house of someone who has nothing to do with architecture or design—a lawyer, for instance—you'll see they have top-class furnishings. It's because they've internalised it.

AA We're still a long way from achieving that normality.

RE I think that what Ramón was saying about Italy is starting to happen here. People now appreciate having a good piece of modern furniture.

AA The first thing is to teach them to distinguish what a good piece is.

RE That's the beginning of culture. It's always the way.

AA It's a small market, but it's improved. I know it first hand because my wife has a shop that sells twentieth-century antiques. It's called Tiempos Modernos, and she opened it in 1988. The office I set up on the top floor of my mother's house was furnished with the pieces from the fifties that she didn't manage to sell. It was just impossible… Fortunately, tastes have changed greatly since then, and the shop has worked well. People have indeed learned and now know how to choose. They'll now spend a certain amount on a piece of furniture, which is never as much as all that.

RE The democratisation of design has helped to introduce that culture to every sector, in terms of both age and income. It now really exists in a part of society that's been educated with affordable but well designed pieces, which means that when they acquire more spending power, they look for modern pieces of a higher calibre. There are certain parallels with what's happening in the fashion world.

AA Yes. That world has some positive values right now.

RE However, I think we sometimes need a basic substratum of knowledge, even if it's of furniture of lesser quality, for that new culture to emerge from it. In other words, the existence of something like Zara makes people dress well, but when someone acquires more spending power, they buy Prada, Dior or Yves Saint Laurent. Without that minimal cultural basis, the difference is too extreme.

AA Luxury stores are for the few.

RE But there has to be some kind of recognition. It's a question of aspirations. The copy sometimes gives the original its value, but for design to be given that value, there has to be a society that already understands what it is. Even if it can't buy it straight off, it must be able to appreciate it.

AA Society needs coaching, is that it?

RE It's a kind of coaching. We go from the close and affordable to the remote and inaccessible but desirable. It must be understood to be valued. It's a process.

AA Yes, yes. That's changed a great deal. Taste has to do with education, but also with economic status.

RE Cultural level and economic status are what generate value for design. If you don't have both—that is, if there's money but no culture—then we don't progress, either.

RÚ Selling a book by Chema Madoz or Alberto García-Alix must be very similar to selling a piece of choice furniture. Is it the same public that buys certain furnishings and also buys these books?

AA Well, I think taste is all-embracing. A person with taste generally has it for art, for furniture, for clothes, for where they eat—which doesn't have to be precisely the most expensive place.

RE Of course. The most expensive things are not always the ones that most satisfy you, and they're not always the best. With good judgement, you can find very good things for a smaller outlay.

AA Which is the piece you've most liked doing?

RE I've liked lots of them. The first ones that come into my head are the Vondom daybeds, because it's a piece on such a large scale that you're almost on the borderline between architecture and furnishing. They're like big loungers for two or three people, and they've moreover proved very popular. The first one, the Faz daybed, appeared naturally, as the piece had to be added to the collection. Now, the daybeds are one of the pieces that most identify the brand. It's not easy to do that, even when you try, and these pieces have always differentiated us.

AA That doesn't only happen with furniture. It's very difficult these days—at least for me, since I'm not an expert—to differentiate one car from another, for example.

RÚ But you do differentiate the very good ones.

AA Yes, of course, the classics.

RE Even the contemporary ones. When they're very good, you say, 'This one's got something…'.

AA But you notice that even the most important brands have to go with the flow a little, as a culture has been created. I get the impression that happens with furniture as well.

RE Possibly. The origin of those daybeds was that they were designed on the basis of extremely pure geometry. It's true, however, that when you have to produce more, you look at the market and the current trends condition you, something I found hard to recognise at first.

AA There's a culture which ultimately obliges you to do that.

RE My starting point is never a trend, but in the process of investigation and conceptualisation, we do a study of related products. That prevents you from getting left out. Even if unconsciously, that information influences you. It happens with fashion too. There comes a point when you realise you've been left out.

AA The thing is that in the world of clothing, there's been a phenomenon of popularisation that has also been fundamental to design.

RE The democratisation of fashion and design. That's a fact, and I think it's a good thing.

AA Can you see yourself designing something very popular and therefore very cheap?

RE A lot of pieces have become elitist because we produce them in very small series and with very high costs. Nearly all the ones I've designed have been in that category, and I think it's a privilege to be able to design something with brands that can reach everyone.

P. 64

HAND-DRAWN OR MACHINE-DRAWN ?

NOTEBOOK

For centuries, drawing by hand has been the origin of every project. On tablets, parchments or papers, with a graver, pencil or pen. At the start of the 1990s, however, a meteoric revolution took place. Methods of drawing with computer programs appeared, instantly and almost insultingly displacing manual draughtsmanship.

Ramón Esteve belongs to the hinge generation of designers who were educated in the virtues of the pencil but had no qualms about riding the digital wave when it hit them. They are proficient at both techniques, combining the best of each. His skill at manual drawing, which he had practised since he was a child and nearly persuaded him to enrol as a fine arts student, has allowed him to transfer his offspring, whether furniture or buildings, directly from the idea in his mind onto the paper.

Nowadays, it is possible to be a great designer with scarcely any ability to draw. However, it is also true that those who have continued to produce hand-drawn sketches manage to retain a personality of their own that machine processes tend to efface. Pixels put everyone on the same level. The hand, man's best friend, is nevertheless singular and unique. It is an extraordinary instrument that truly and swiftly converts neurons into signs and ideas into documents.

The stroke of each hand has its own peculiar force. No two hands are the same. We see this in the communicative precision of Foster's drawings, in the trembling and hesitant line of Moneo, in the graffito texture of Mies, in Niemeyer's gestural force, and in the angular and colourful futurism of Hadid.

The bold strokes of Ramón Esteve's sketches and his vaporous and accurate watercolours clearly explain his conceptual intentions: serenity, simplification and forthrightness. Often, the sketch highlights the key that will confer its personality on each piece of furniture. It is the customs seal authorising its materialisation. As a set, his drawings form a nursery of special offspring, a family with the common DNA of the hand that gave birth to them.

P. 66

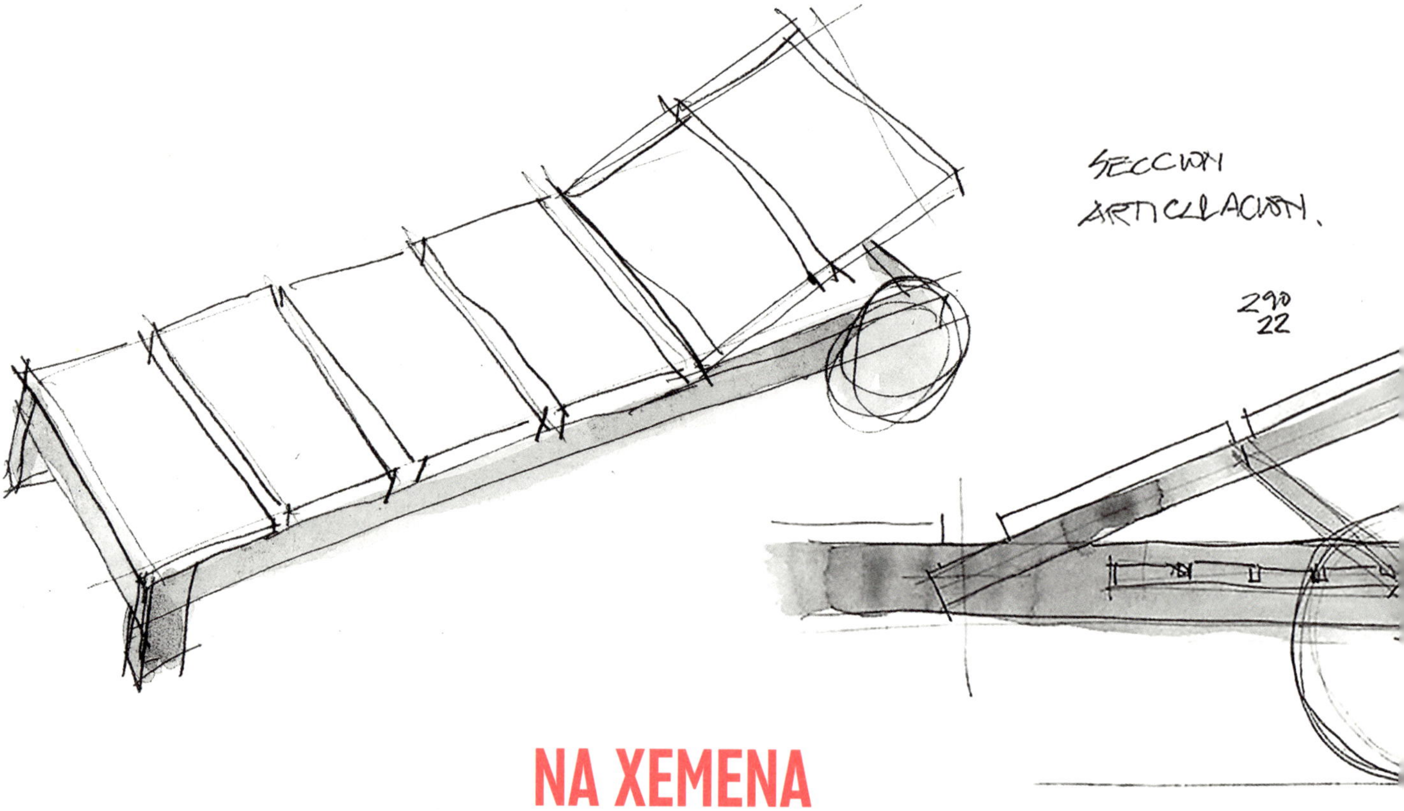

NA XEMENA

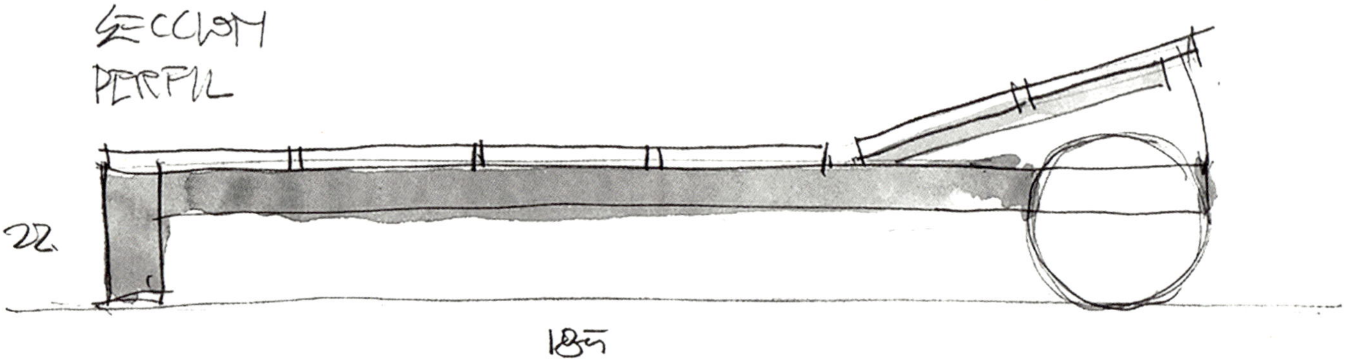

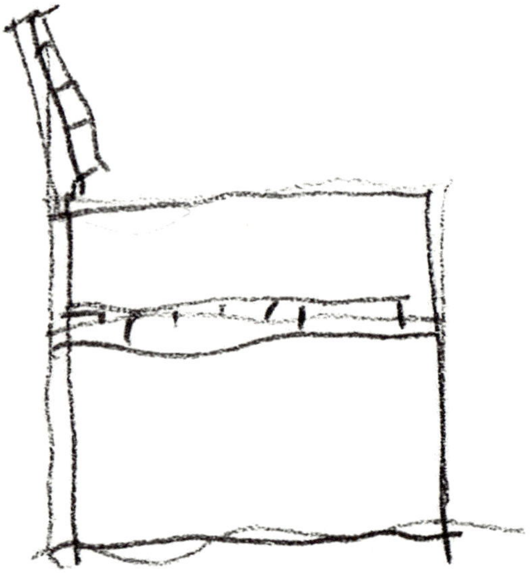

COOL

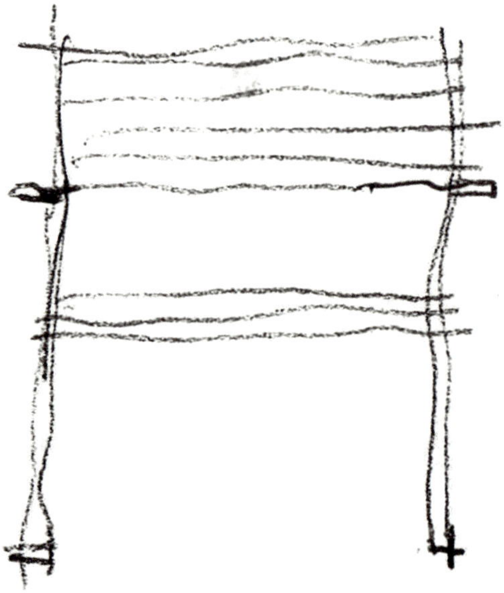

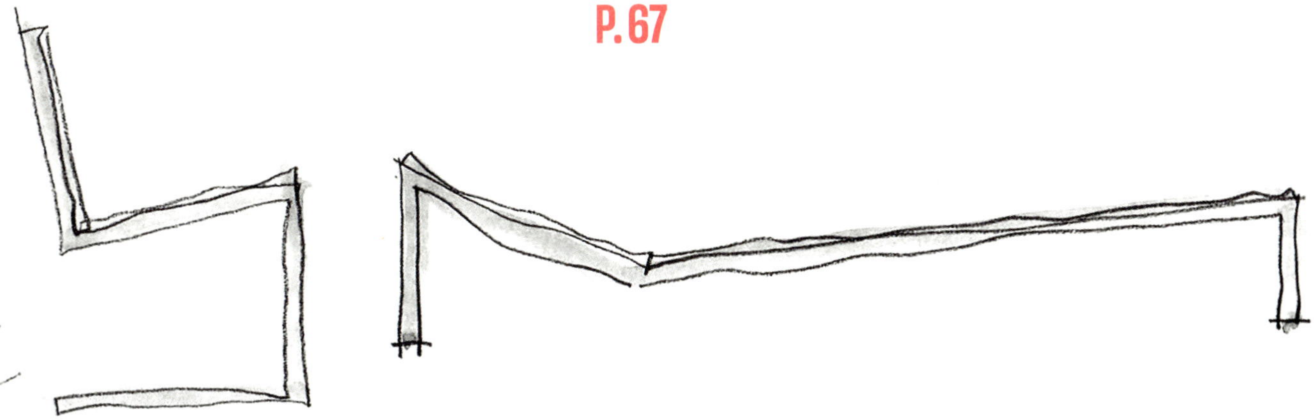

LUNA

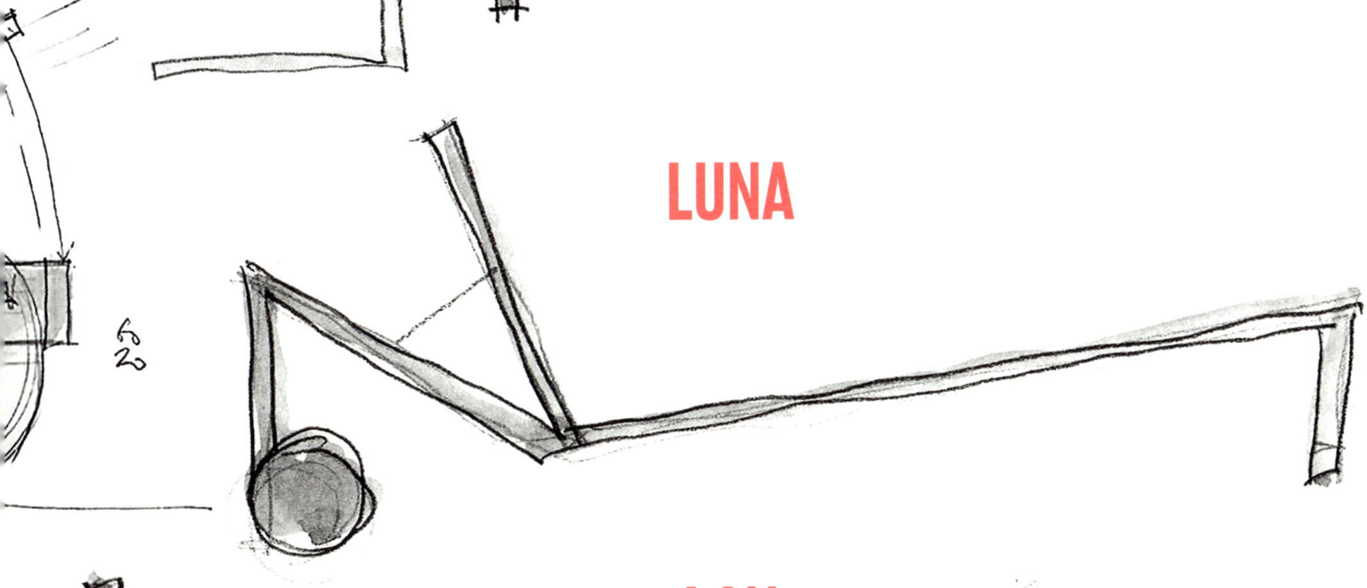

LAN

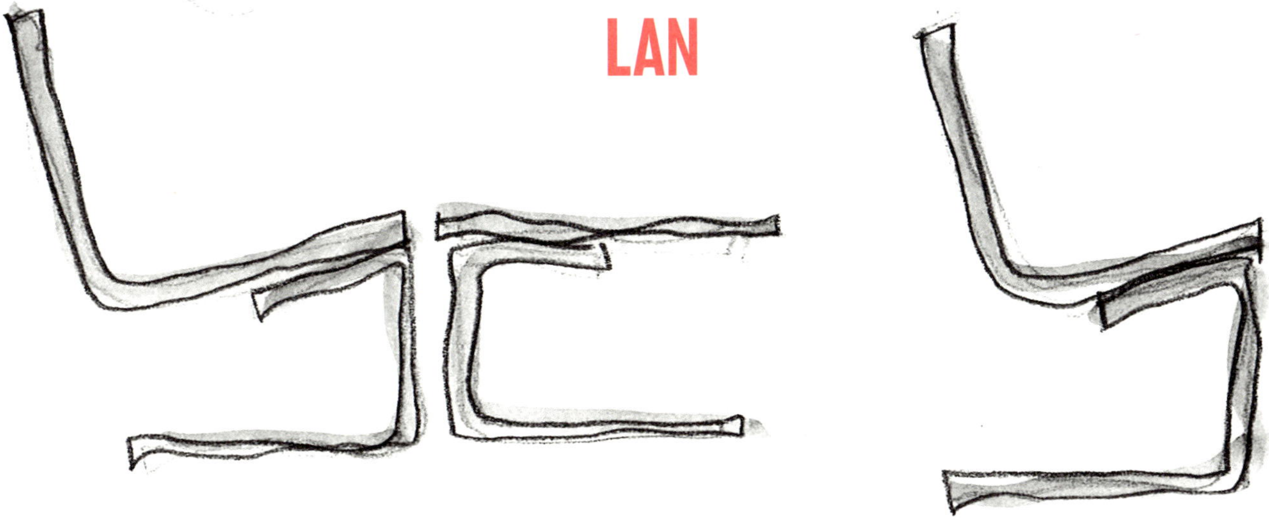

MODO

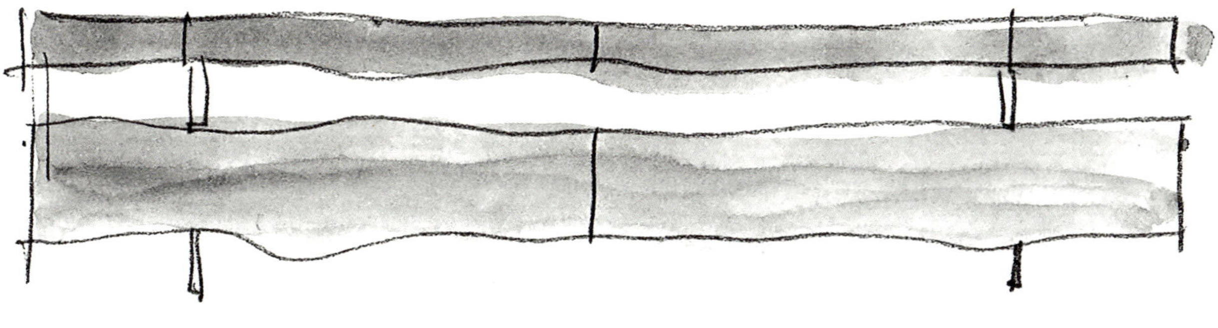

P. 68

PARA

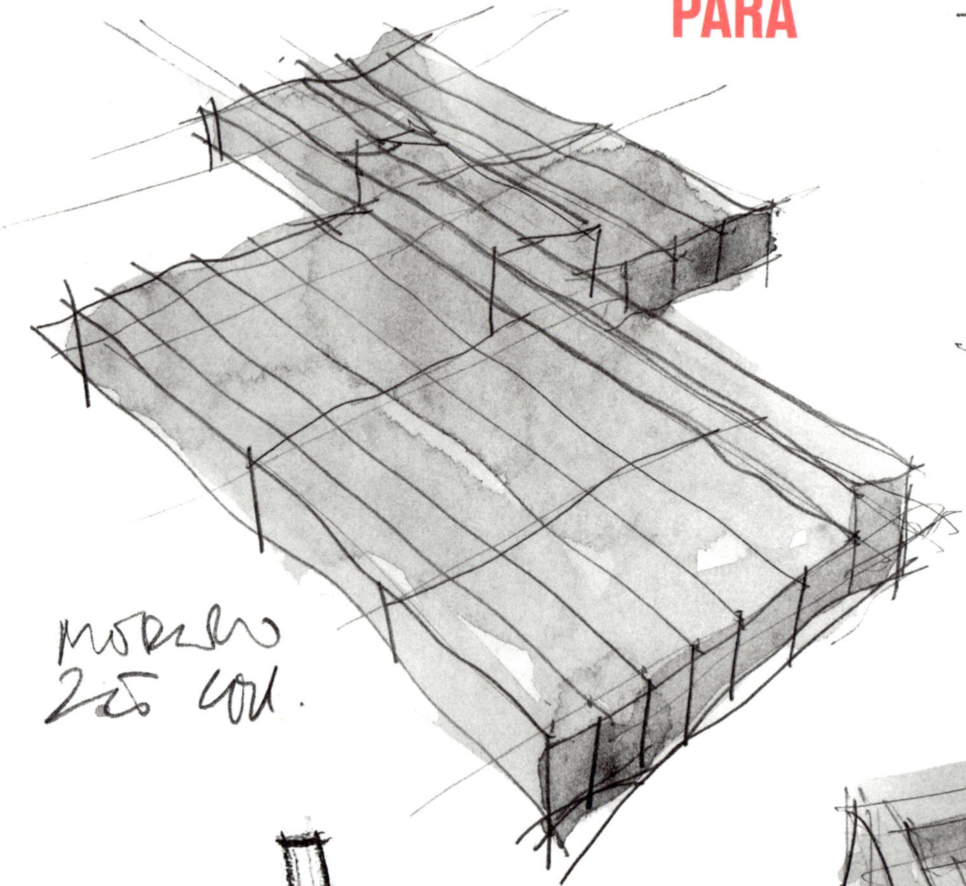

ARC

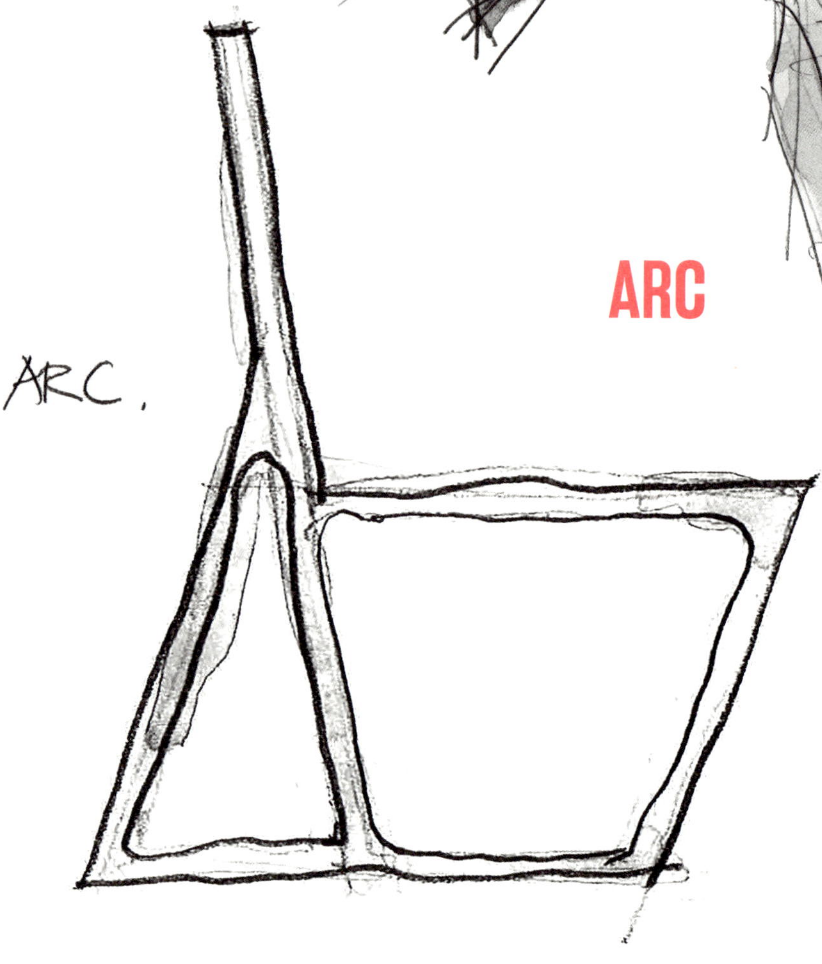

P. 69

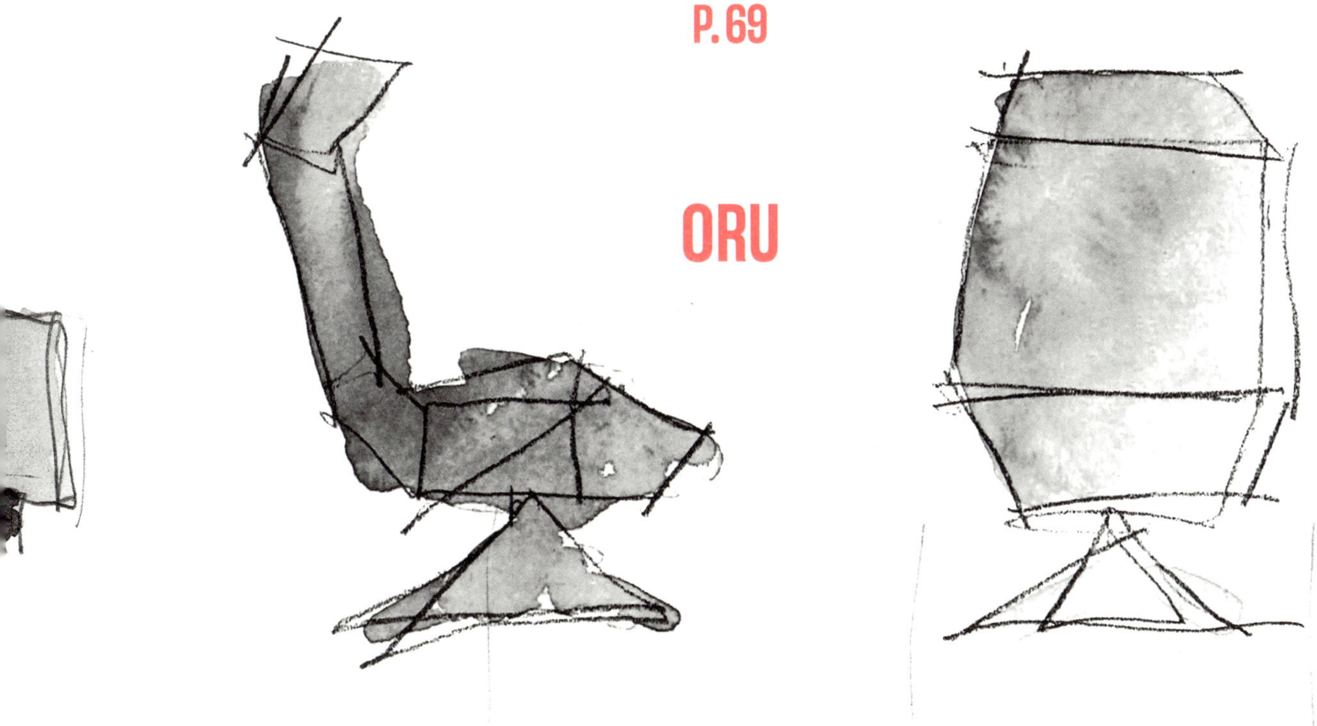

ORU

ORIGAMI

LINK

P.70

CHAISE LONGUE FAZ

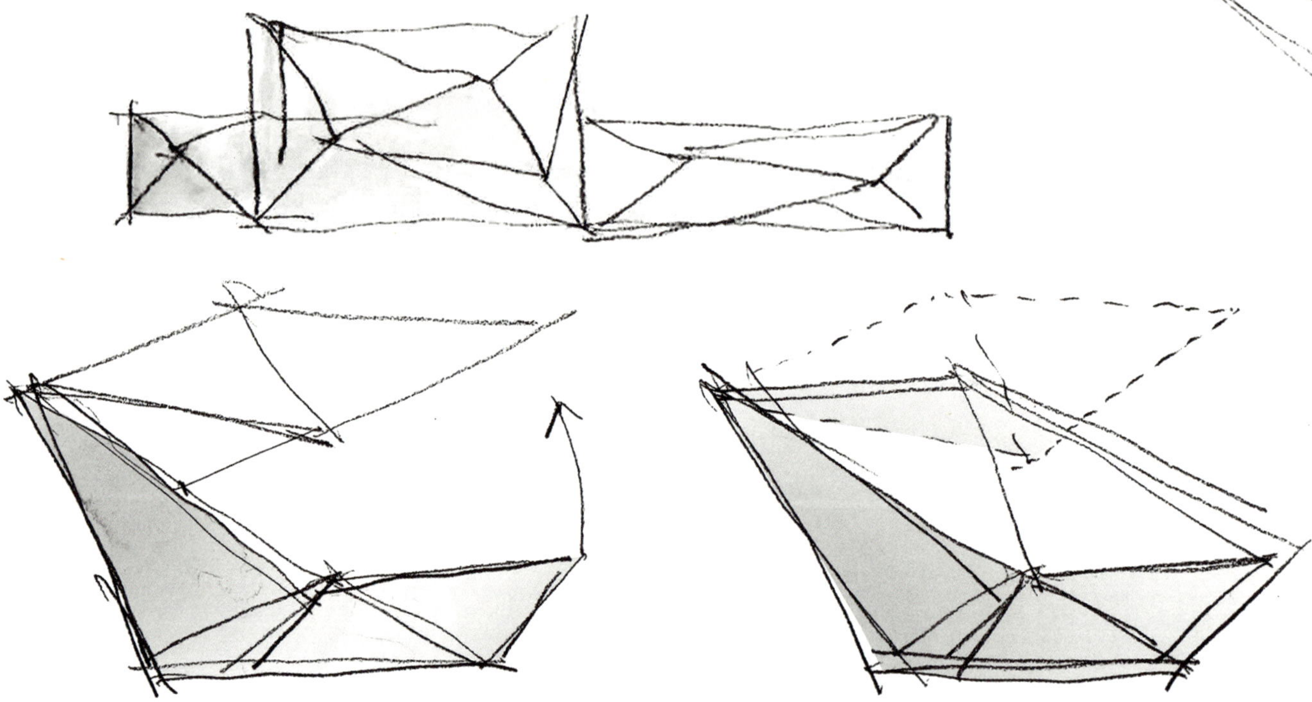

DAYBED FAZ

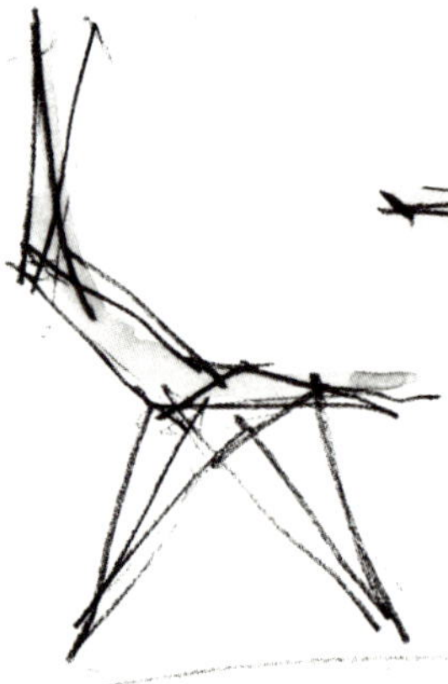

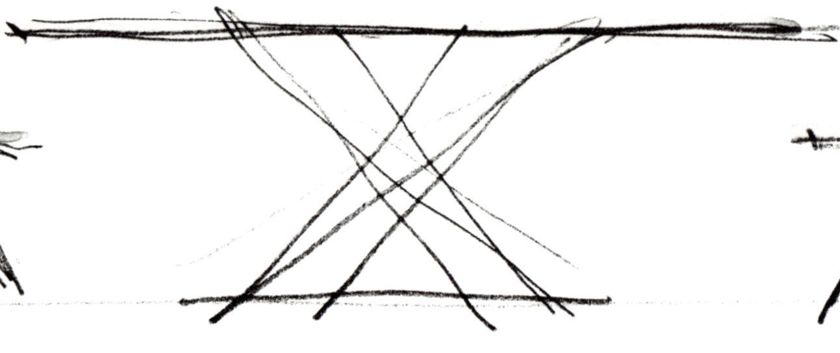

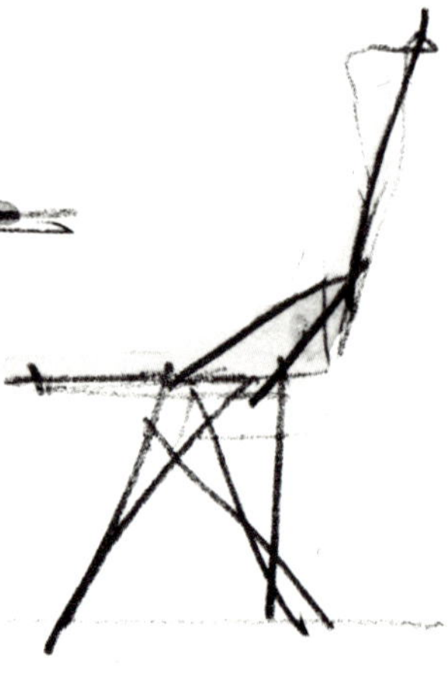

P.71

FAZ CHAIR

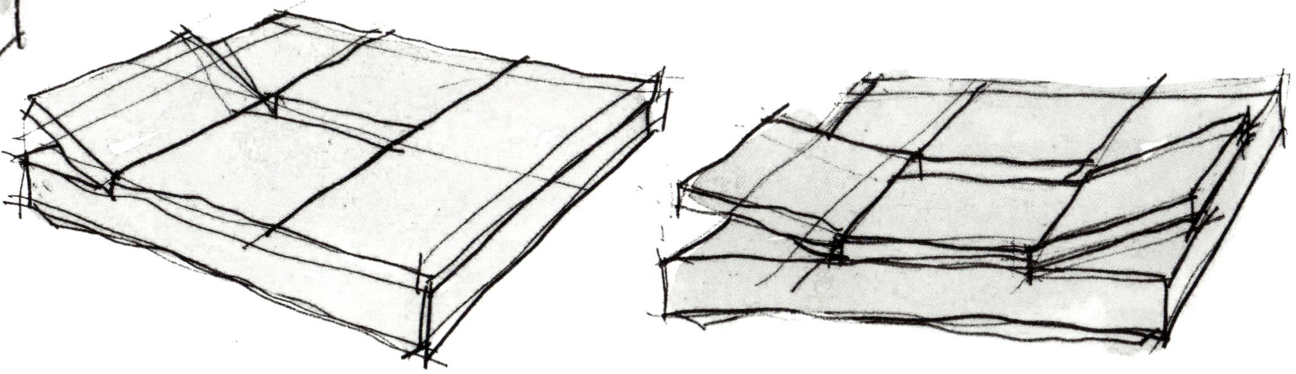

VELA

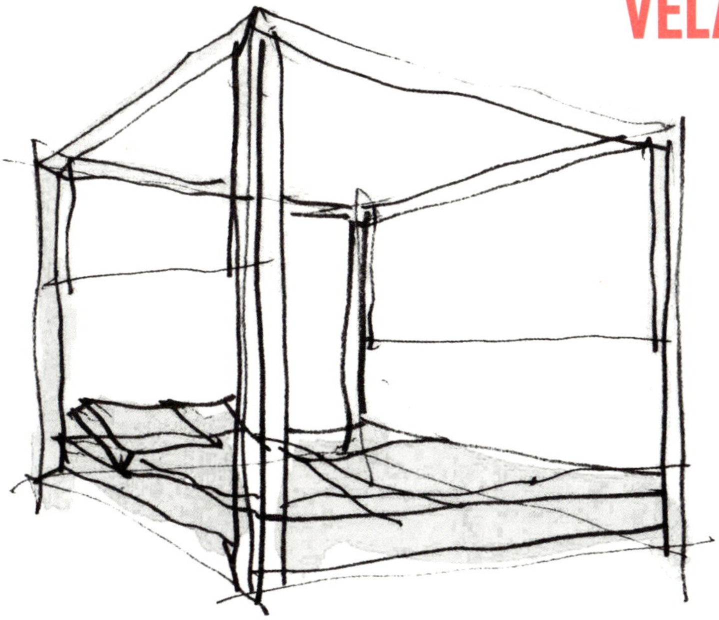

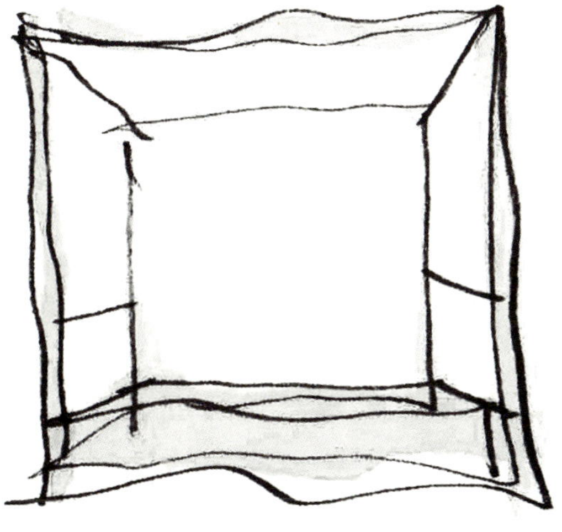

P.72

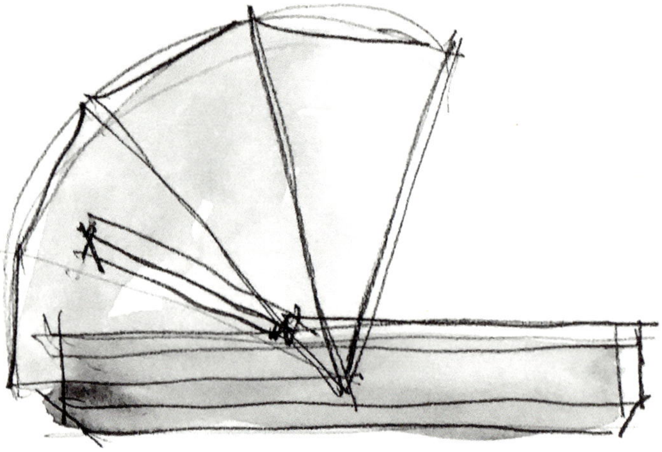

ULM / MOON

TABLET

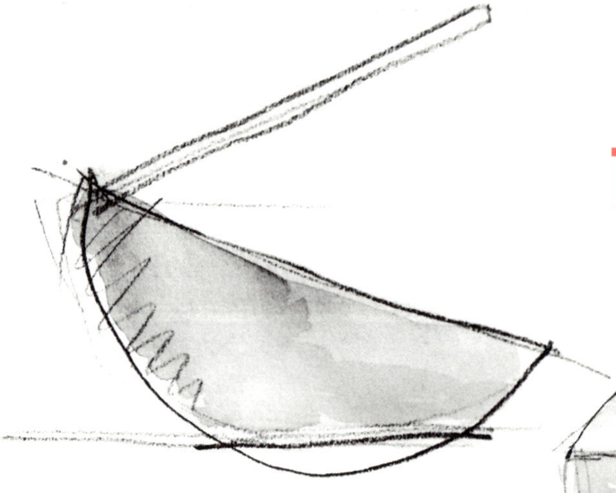

P.73

THESIS

GATSBY

BLACK NOTE

P. 74

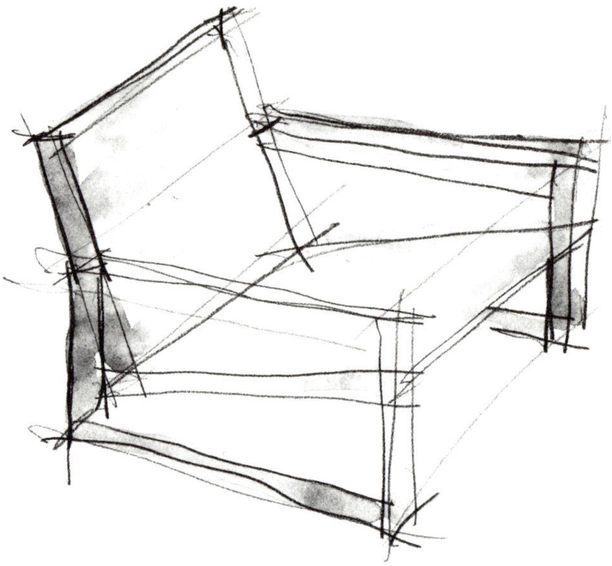

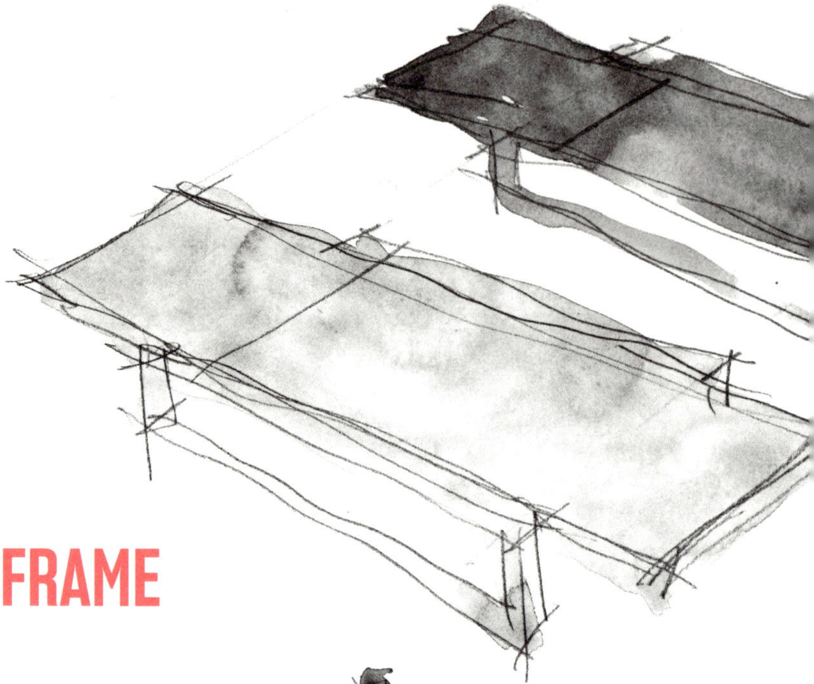

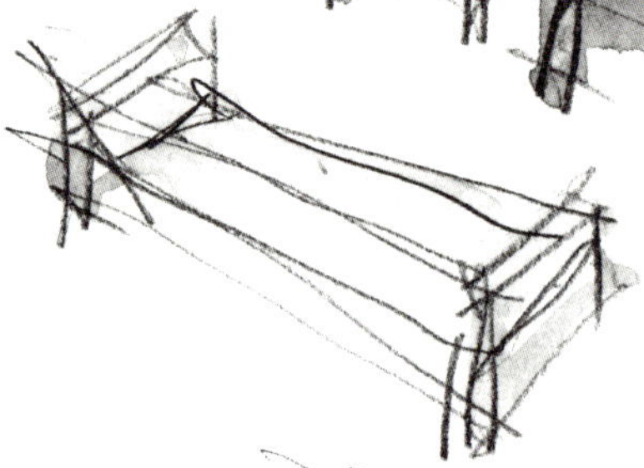

FRAME

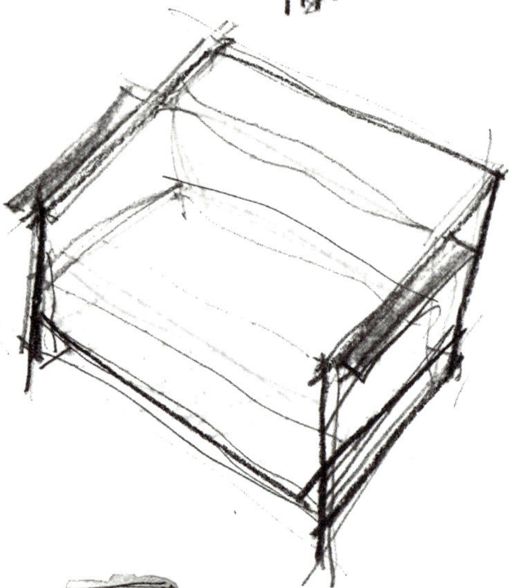

CASILDA

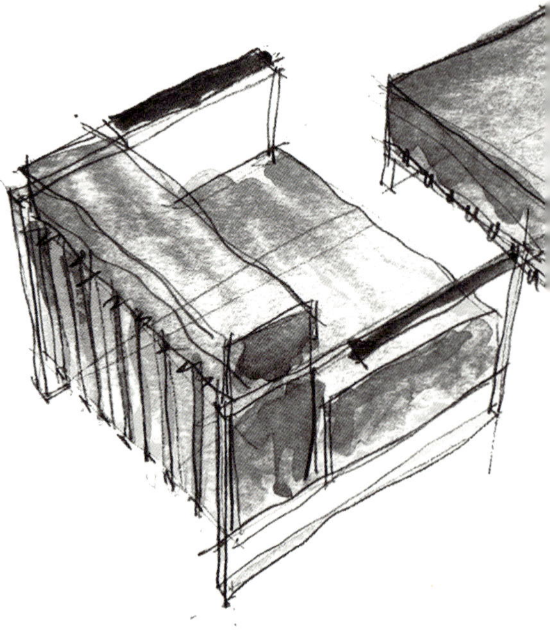

QUARTZ

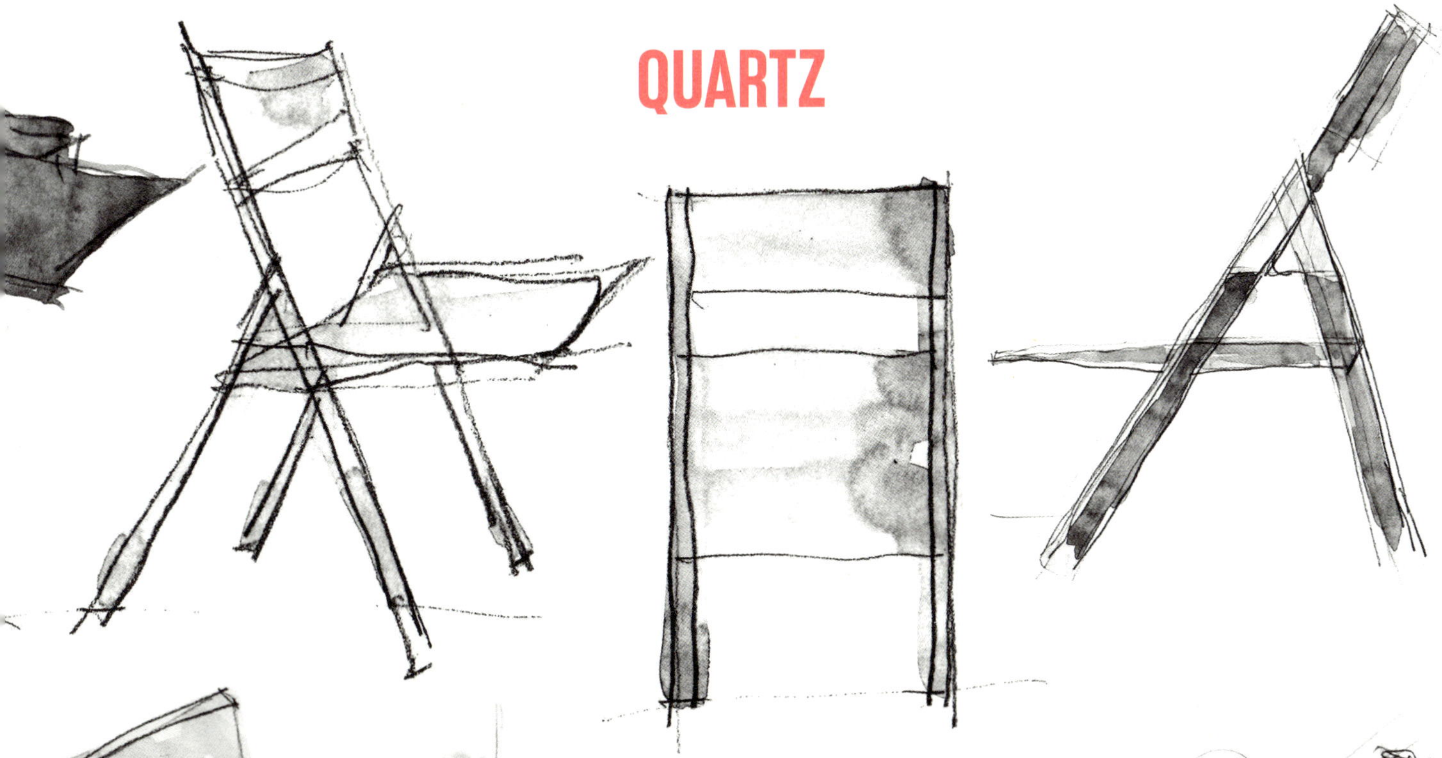

LIGNAGE

PIXEL

P.76

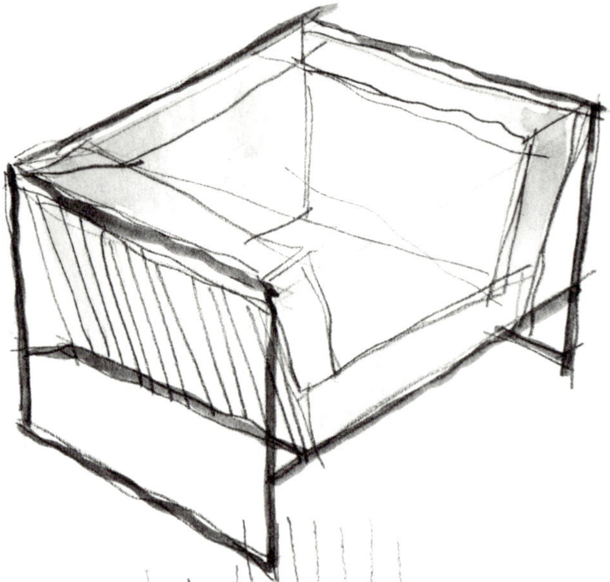

ARPA

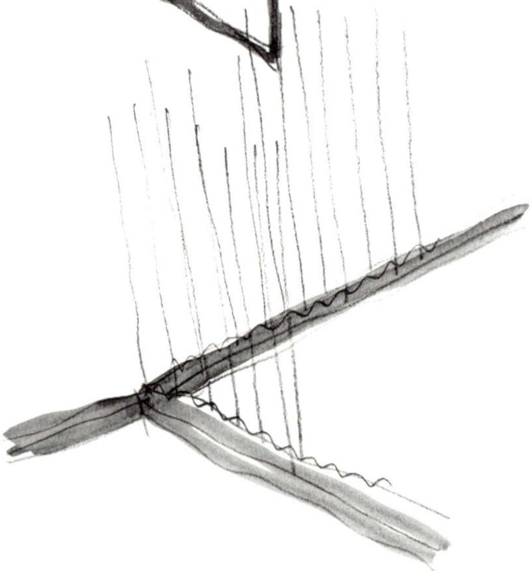

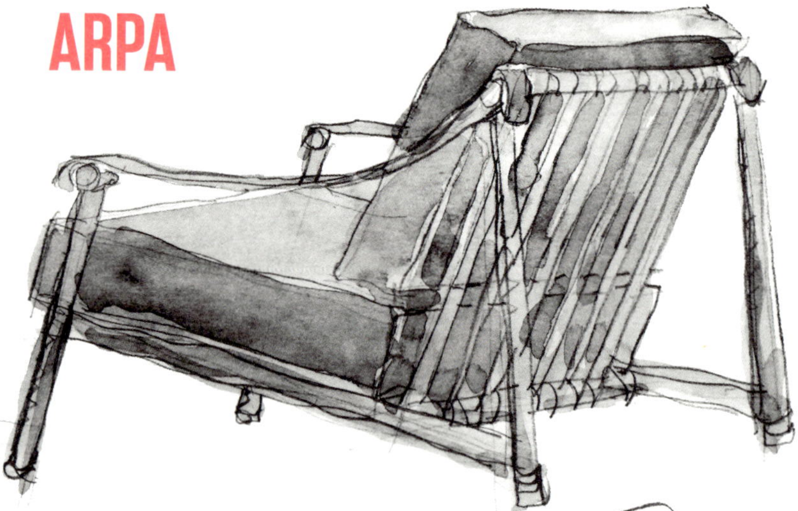

HUDSON

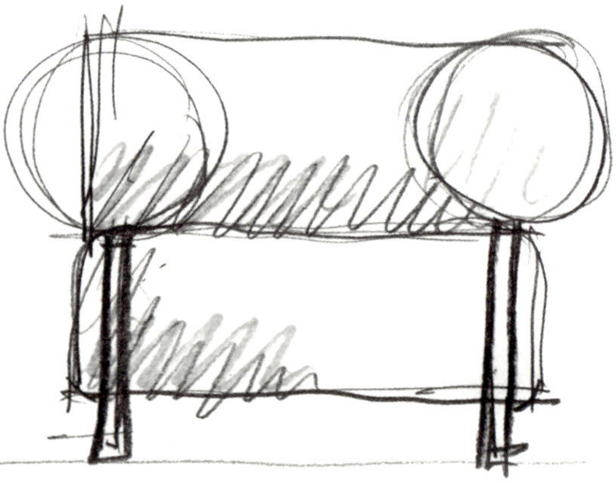

JUMBO

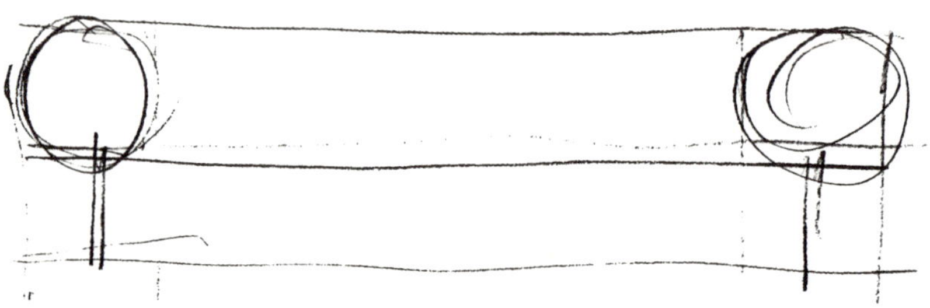

P.77

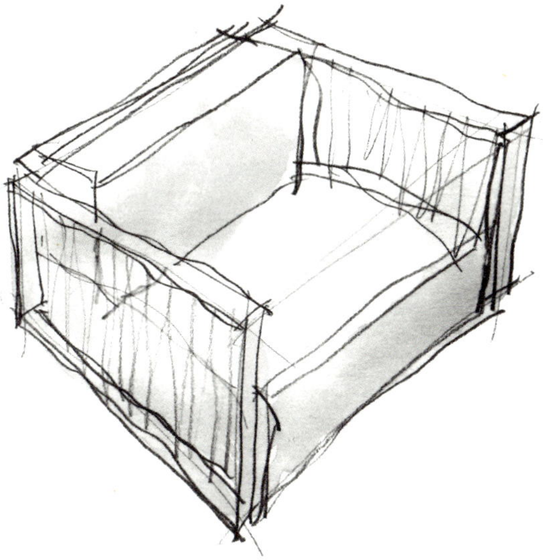

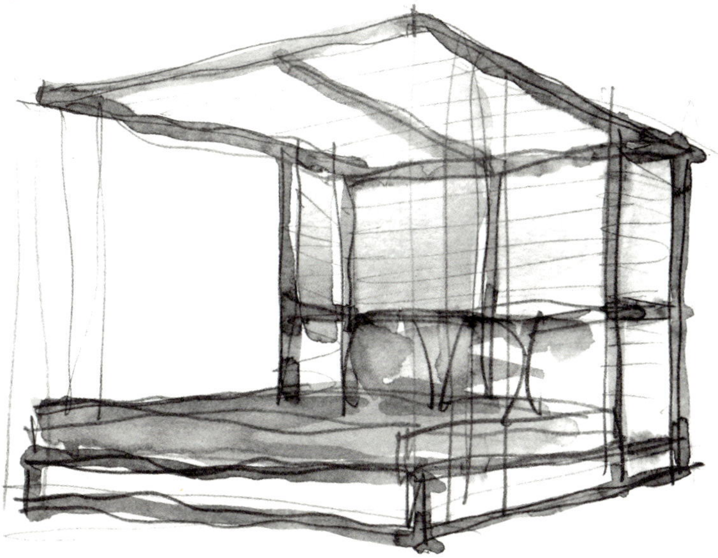

THE FACTORY

VINEYARD

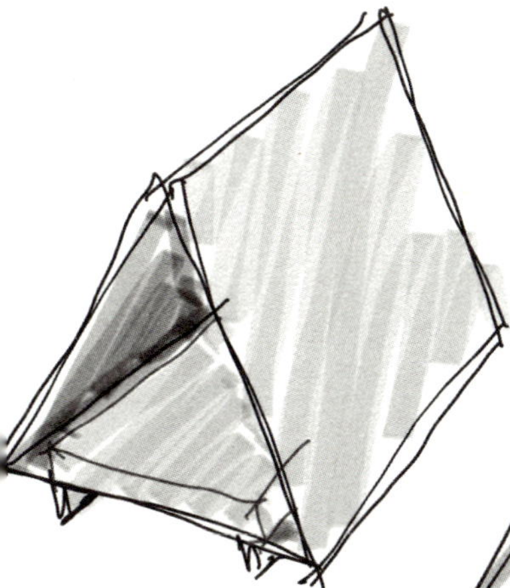

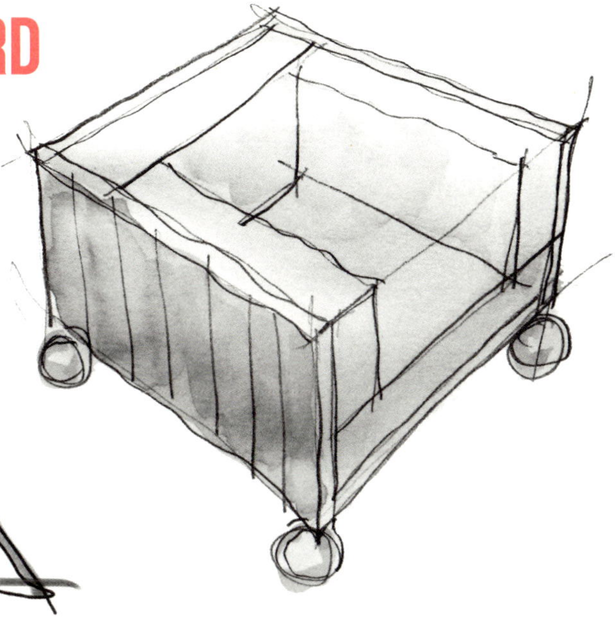

P. 78

TEMPO

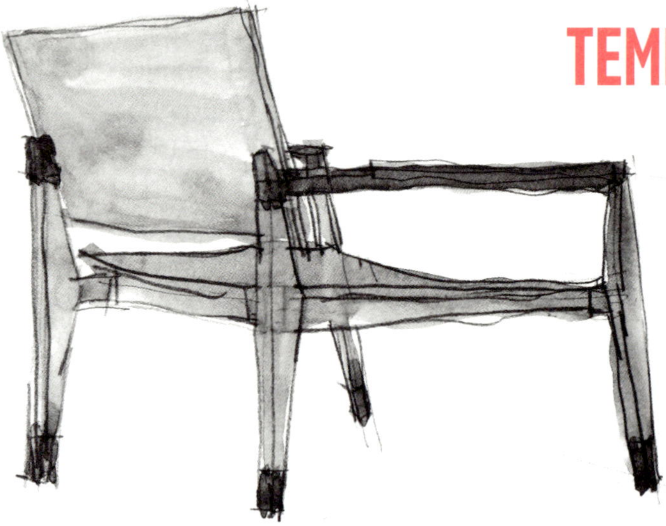

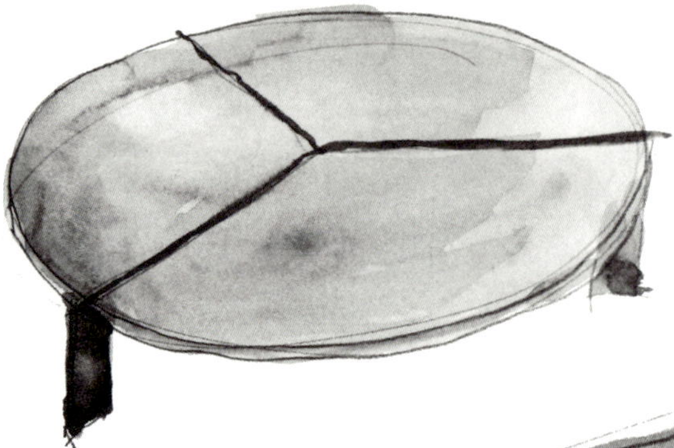

MITJORN

HAMPTONS

P.79

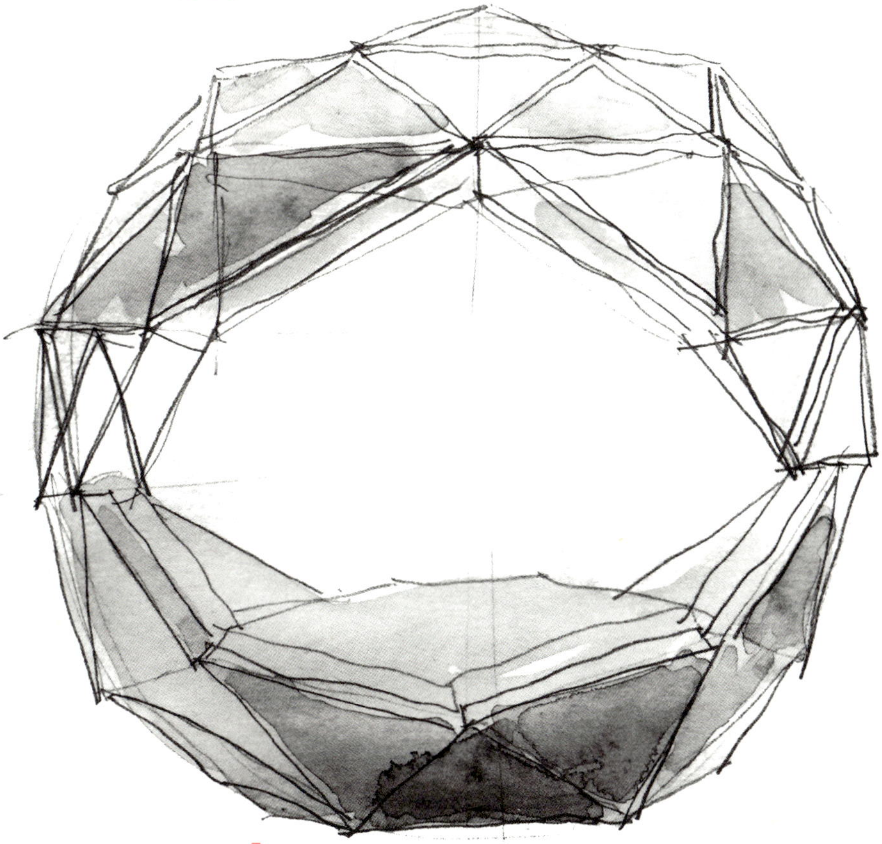

IGLÚ

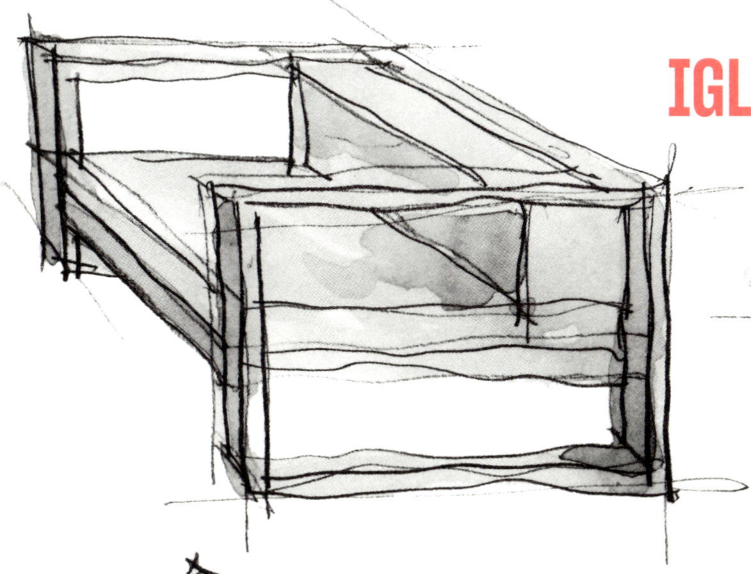

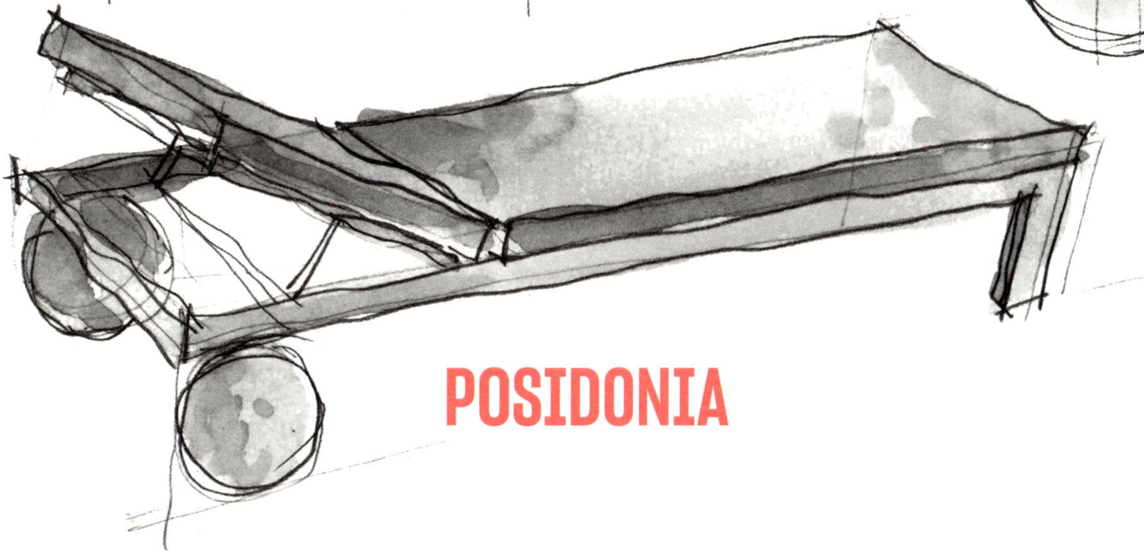

POSIDONIA

P. 80

CHRONOLOGY

1996—2023

1996

Mario Vargas Llosa joints the Real Academia Española (RAE) / François Miterrand dies / José María Aznar wins the elections with the conservative Partido Popular for the first time / Mad cow disease appears / Atlanta Olympics / First artificial heart implant.

NA XEMENA
Gandia Blasco

There is always a first time. This lounge chair was the first piece of furniture designed by Ramón Esteve. It started as a personal need to provide coherent furnishings for the house he was designing in Ibiza. Not finding what he wanted on the market was the incentive, as is the case with many other architects, which drove him to create his own repertoire. He inadvertently gave birth to an icon: the outdoor Mediterranean lounger *par excellence*. This is because of its structure, radical aesthetics, modern support surface and characteristic wheels. It was quite fortunate that he got everything so absolutely right in his first project of the kind. Many copies followed it from then on, and a new creative facet of his studio—furniture design—got under way. It was to be of crucial importance for his development.

Na Xemena House

1999

The single currency in the European Union enters into force / Michael Jordan leaves the NBA / Pedro Almodóvar wins an Oscar for the film *All About my Mother* / Last solar eclipse in the millennium / The reality show Big Brother premieres in the Netherlands / John Paul II starts the Great Jubilee of 2000.

COOL
Gandia Blasco

The success of the Na Xemena lounger led to the ambitious challenge of designing a complete collection of outdoor furniture. An exercise in efficient simplicity. It involves a reduction to the minimum of the square-sectioned load-bearing steel structure, which supports the wooden or polyethylene slats that give it order and direction. This pattern is applied to the chair, tables and lounger, creating a comfortable metal grid that seems to float in space. Every piece is a word that rhymes with the others, articulating a language that is recognisably ancient and familiar but which here appears contemporary and timeless.

FROM THE CREATIVE POINT OF VIEW, AS A DESIGNER, MY STUDIO IS CLOSER TO A CRAFTSMAN'S WORKSHOP THAN A FIRM.

—

I EASED QUITE NATURALLY INTO DESIGNING OUTDOOR FURNISHINGS. IN FACT, I'VE BEEN CATALOGUED WITHIN THE SPECIALITY. WHAT I REALLY DID WAS TO REPRODUCE THE INTERIOR PROGRAMME OF THE HOUSE ON THE EXTERIOR.

HAND TUFTED
Gandia Blasco

For an architect, a carpet is not a plane but a three-dimensional surface with thickness, texture, relief and colouring, which is not flat but volumetric. It manifests itself through the type of pile and loop, with its shadows, moiré and folds. These carpets are inspired by and evoke cities that have been experienced. Each one tells of the journey to a distant city, while at home it serves to delimit an expressive territory, a comfortable platform to tread on, and a canvas to be enjoyed.

2000

The computer virus ILoveYou paralyses millions of computers all over the world / Ridley Scott releases the film *Gladiator* / China reaches an agreement with the EU to open its market / The cloning of human embryos for medical purposes is approved.

BABIA
Gandia Blasco

The dream of every designer is to found his own production company. Aalto did so with Artek, Tusquets with BD, and many others have tried. It means the freedom to be able to decide. To produce his creations, Ramón Esteve set up a firm with Pablo Gironés, which was eventually integrated into Gandía Blasco. That is the origin of Babia, a bedroom collection, a living-room suite, and a set of mirrors. Pure forms, elementary geometry, all in consonance with the architectural works he was developing at that time. And a seedbed for what would come later.

The Tower House

2003

Design Year is held in Spain / United States invades Iraq / Last Concorde flight / Belgium recognises same-sex marriages / Dolly the sheep dies / Apple opens the iTunes store / Arnold Schwarzenegger becomes the governor of California / Greta Thunberg is born.

LUNA
Gandia Blasco

An exercise in taking earlier outdoor furnishing designs to their limits based on the studio's own décor for the Luna Café. The structure is stylised still further, and there is an unexpected shift in the design of the lounge chair. These are pieces that have sprung directly from the drawing board, like a happy accident. The innovation consists of using shiny methacrylate plates, which gives the pieces a singular effect of transparency and lightness. Hitherto unseen, such a form of expression takes a firm leap into colour with neoclassicist connotations.

Flat in the city

LE CORBUSIER: 'ARCHITECTURE IS THE MASTERLY, CORRECT AND MAGNIFICENT PLAY OF MASSES BROUGHT TOGETHER IN LIGHT.' IT'S SOMETHING ALEATORY, YET BOUND BY CERTAIN RULES THAT LEAVE ROOM FOR CREATIVITY AND SPONTANEITY.

—

A GOOD DESIGN IS ONE THAT DOESN'T LOOK AS THOUGH IT'S BEEN DESIGNED. IT'S THERE, WITHOUT SHOUTING. GOOD DESIGN ISN'T PERCEPTIBLE, IT'S IN HARMONY WITH ITS CONTEXT WHILE IT'S FULFILLING ITS FUNCTION.

2004

NASA's Spirit rover lands on Mars / Mark Zuckerberg launches Facebook / Paul Buchheit creates Gmail / 11 March terrorist attack / Zapatero is elected president of Spain / Athens Olympics / Messi debuts on Barça at the age of seventeen.

PARA
Joquer

The first incursion into home furnishing for indoor use. These are two totally different pieces, both forthright, one heavy and the other weightless. They are presented with a radical force and professionalism.

The *chaise longue*, a classic exercise of great architects from Le Corbusier to the Eames, Mies, or Aalto, is resolved with perfect sinuosity. It floats gracefully in the space. In the meantime, a parallelepiped elementary structure merely pushes and sustains it without itself being exhibited. The ten supporting pads offer themselves like welcoming vertebrae on which to settle. Sacrilegious as it may sound, it is an improvement on the Soft Pad that the Eames made for Billy Wilder.

On the other hand, the collection of sofas represents gravity, mass, and orderly and logical volume. The detail of the curve on each pad, concomitant with the *chaise longue*, turns the cube into a mattress and announces its comfort. The strip motif gives it a pre-eminent linear component. While sofas are usually segmented into vertical sections to indicate units, the strips here run parallel to the back, making for a perception analogous to paving or the architectural composition of the space itself.

It is curious to see how the sketches of this system of sofas could be taken as arrangements of buildings, harmonious volumes, whether house or object, in search of their best spatial composition.

Carmen House Studio

2004

MODO
Joquer

This is an elementary design with great spatial potency. On a compact and geometrically pure base, a light enveloping volume appears to levitate, as if it were a satellite revolving around the base. Evidently, it is anchored—and strongly, too. It rests on a chrome steel frame, but one that is scarcely noticeable, with a certain magic to the way it displays the parallel volumes, especially the end corners. It is a touch that bestows power on the whole piece.

The subtle structure is certainly beautiful but, above all, it is rational—or it is beautiful for precisely that reason. From the front, it is barely seen, as the edge vanishes among reflections, and from the side, it looks potent and robust, with an appearance of solidity.

Lemon Tree House

PAR
Joquer

Cube = volume. The cube is the archetypal form of volume, most of all for an architect. It represents the elementary space, the basis of any construction, and the unit of spatial measurement—the three dimensions *x*, *y* and *z*. In addition, however, the cube as a seat has also been a recurrent motif for architects when designing armchairs, like Hoffmann's Kubus, Gropius's armchair, or the famous Grand Confort of Charlotte Perriand, signed by Le Corbusier. Par is an exercise on this theme, but a lighter variation for an upright chair instead of an armchair, where the legs and seat are going to share the volume between them. In the bottom half, the side legs have remained in the form of runners but with a considerable thickness that makes for solidity, simultaneously clearing the base of material. That material rests above, on the top half, aesthetically outlined without showing any difference between the back and the arms, and merely hollowing out the seat. That is exactly the typological key: radically reducing the volume on the upper level without allowing the back, always a discordant element, to protrude. In this way, a compositional purity is achieved that functions well when the pieces are repeated or lined up. Like boxes resting on boxes. Moreover, colour is used to add dynamism to the furniture.

THINGS LOSE VALUE WHEN THERE IS NO CONTENT. IT IS A TRANSCENDENTAL QUESTION THAT CAN BE APPLIED TO NEARLY ALL DISCIPLINES.

—

A DESIGNER ISN'T NECESSARILY AN ARTIST, EITHER. WANTING TO DESIGN AS IF YOU WERE AN ARTIST, OR THINKING YOU ARE AN ARTIST, IS SOMETHING I DON'T GO ALONG WITH. HOWEVER, THE CREATIONS OCCASIONALLY GO FURTHER THAN WHAT THEY BASICALLY ARE.

2005

Charles of Wales announces his wedding with Camila Parker / Windsor Tower in Madrid catches fire / YouTube is launched / Gary Kasparov retires from chess / Astronomers see the light of planets outside the solar system for the first time / Joseph Ratzinger succeeds John Paul II as Pope Benedict XVI.

VANO
Joquer

The Vano sofa is the mother of the Par chair. The cubic tradition is distorted to achieve comfortable measurements for a sofa, whose composition is always marked by horizontality. The mass is signalled in two parts with a subtly insinuated cut that breaks the linearity and marks the two seating units. Once more, there is no difference between the back and arm, and the structure continues around the sides. However, its mass is compensated by the structure that lifts it off the ground and lets the flooring in. The armchair version is shaped like the radically cubic design in the Par collection, as commented on below.

LAN
Upoh

The challenge consists of revising the history of the modern chair and, more specifically, the cantilever chair designed by Mart Stam, although it was Breuer and Mies who put their signature on it and refined it.

Here, an extra twist is given to the system, which is born from a very simple sketch. What happens if the structure is detained precisely where the cantilever prevents it from tipping over? The formal novelty lies there, where the seat of the chair is left dangling, free of all support, yet stable. And comfortable, too, as the flexibility of the steel gives it a gentle sway. Laying the backrest on the edge not only optimises it in structural terms but permits greater expression in the mouldings, especially the upper one, by reducing the 90° of the right angle.

Another feature is that the seat and backrest are given a very fine but generously curved profile, making it impossible to pinpoint where one ends and the other begins. It is clearly a chair in the modern style but softened by an organic touch.

The stackable model, with four legs, renounces these svelte forms but solves a difficult problem with great skill by ensuring its stackability is not so obvious that it spoils the model.

Solana House

ORU
Joquer

Continuing the artistic investigation of triangular faceting, having tried it out with plastic, the time now comes to do it on a piece of upholstery. And what better choice than a wingchair—a classic that will allow a little showing off with its configuration. The result is clearly sculptural, like a kind of animal that will embrace and protect you. The unusual base, pentagonal and pyramidal, gives the powerful body that receives you the sturdiness it requires. In their turn, the wings become a generous upper finish that almost forms a protective covering. We could also interpret it as if Arne Jacobsen's famous Egg armchair had been faceted with sliced planes. Once more, a piece of furniture that not only makes us comfortable but becomes one more piece of art in the space it occupies.

House on a slope

ADN
Joquer

The DNA of this sofa is clearly extrusion. It is as if silhouettes had been moulded and extruded to form longitudinal volumes that are then cut up and fitted together. There are two basic pieces, the back and the seat. A third optional one, the footrest, has a longitudinal cut that harmonises with the set and composes an orderly and sedate landscape. Contemplating this sofa evokes the promise of calm and comfort. Moreover, its composition permits combinations to fill large spaces, and it is further enriched with a lower back cushion and a headrest.

2008

Zaragoza Expo 2008 with the slogan 'Water and Sustainable Development' / The Spanish national football team wins the European Cup for the second time / Beijing Olympics / Launch of the Android operating system for mobile phones.

ARC
Upoh

A radical shift in this new furnishing concept. Here, what is explored is wood as the material that generates the idea. For the first time, metal is not the main structural element. This makes it necessary to find the structural essence of wood, which is very variable in its behaviour, toughness and productive process. After analysis and research, it is decided to give full rein to the performative value of the set, with structural knots precisely where the curve—hence the name Arc—is going to nourish the common language of the collection. At the same time, table and chair are conceived as weight-bearing structures of inclined bars, creating a triangulation that dynamises the set. The singular feature is the counter-strut that supports the backrest from behind, a typical detail of architectural reinforcement. There is no doubt this chair was created on the basis of its side elevation, with two silhouettes that are simply propped up by the seat and back.

P.96

WE HAVE TO ACCEPT THE PASSAGE OF TIME IN THE OBJECTS AROUND US. THERE'S A CERTAIN BEAUTY THAT COMES OF AGING.

—

A GOOD CLIENT TELLS YOU WHAT THEY WANT AND WHAT THEY NEED BUT THEN LETS YOU DO IT YOUR OWN WAY.

—

I TRY TO DESIGN SOBER THINGS THAT ARE ALMOST ANONYMOUS, THAT DON'T SEEM TO HAVE ANYONE BEHIND THEM.

2009

Barack Obama becomes President of the United States / Bitcoin is created / Launch of WhatsApp / Michael Jackson dies / U2 holds the first live concert on YouTube / Herta Müller wins the Nobel Prize for Literature.

ORIGAMI
Vibia

The first lighting design, carried out with an innovative system of wall lamps for indoor and outdoor use that broadened what until then had been the limited spectrum of lighting of this kind. As its name indicates, this clear and potent concept evokes the ancient art of paper folding and seeks the subtlety expressed by those folds when illuminated with grazing light. Another attraction of this piece is the infinite number of combinations achieved simply with two moulded fixtures. The fun is combining them so that the light bathes not only the wall but also some part of the neighbouring fixture, resulting in a halo with an enigmatic and atmospheric relief.

Patio House

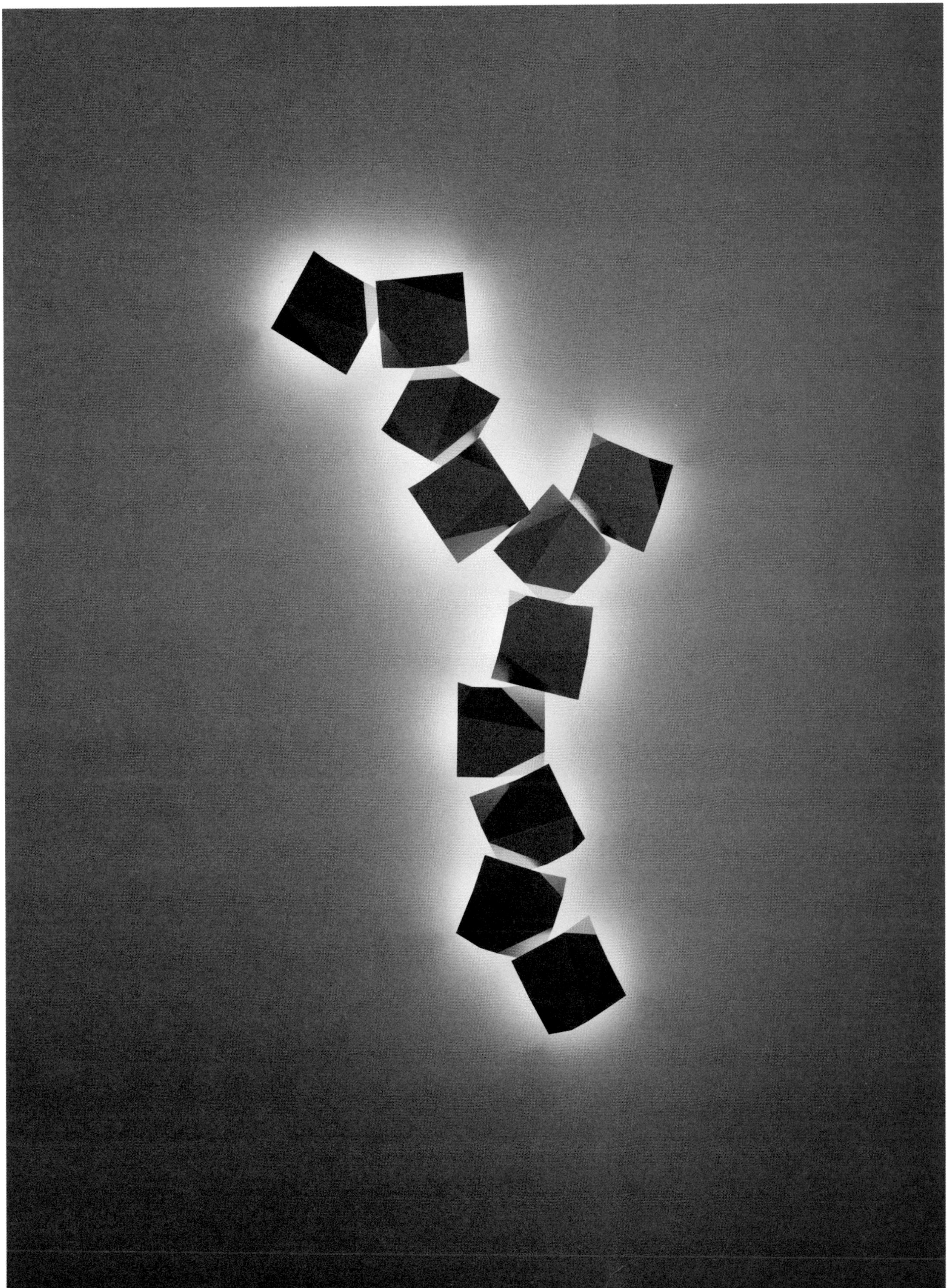

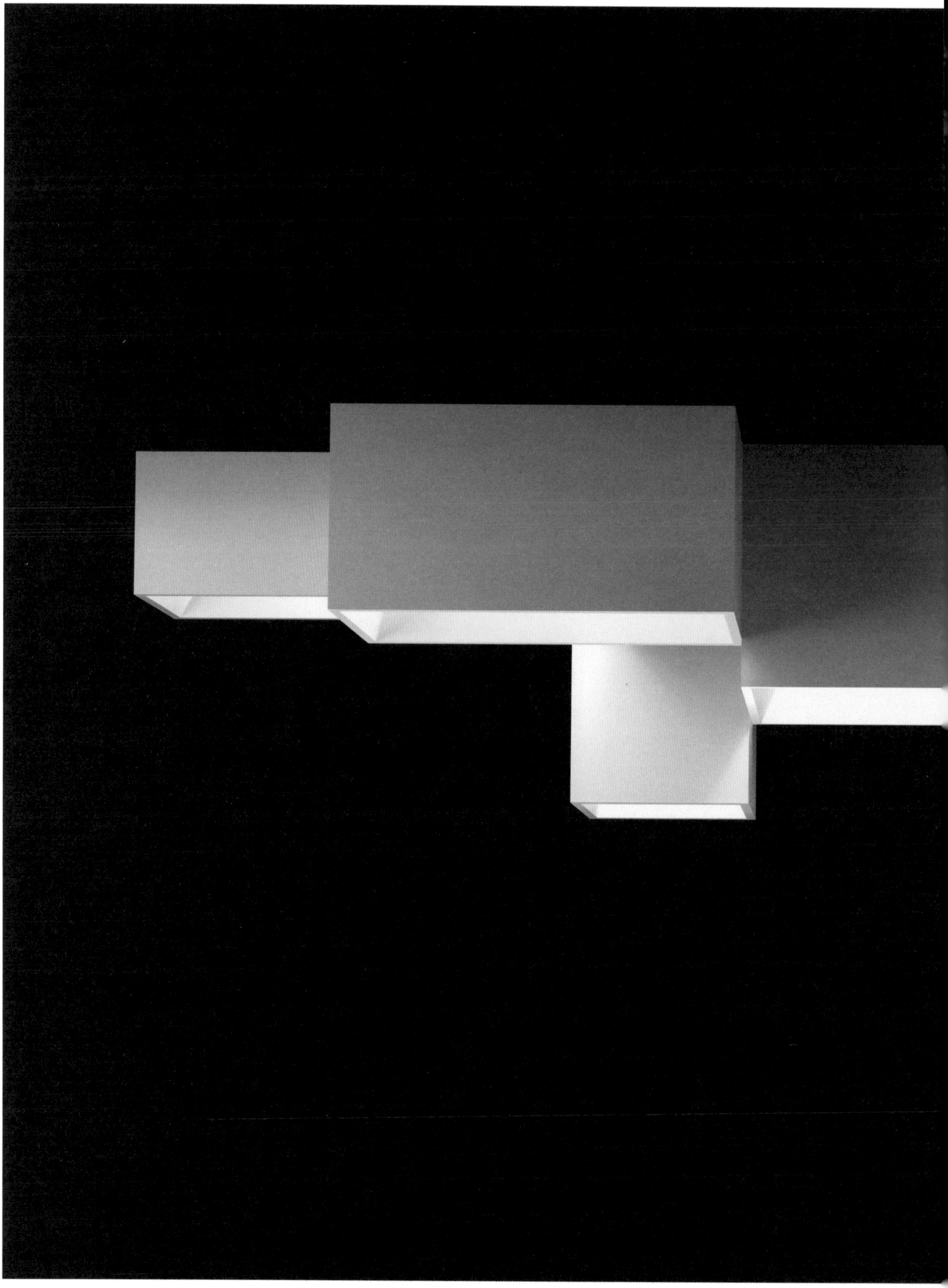

2010

Burj Khalifa in Dubai is inaugurated as the tallest building in the world / Steve Jobs unveils the iPad / José Mujica becomes the President of Uruguay / Spain wins the World Cup in South Africa / Metro-Goldwyn-Mayer declares bankruptcy / Instagram is born.

LINK. LINK XXL
Vibia

An illuminated city hanging from the ceiling. A topsy-turvy world. As such we could describe this unusual lighting system in both its domestic and contract versions. A combined set of different volumes emits pleasantly diffuse light. However, the attraction of these boxes is the optical effect that hides the light source. This magic trick is performed by inclined side panels with the light projected from one side onto the others, removing the source from view. Each box—or building—has different measurements, but its sides will connect onto those of another, making it possible to construct a genuine urban skyline.

The conceptual inspiration for this lamp is clearly architectural. It is based on zenithal skylights, which use different inclinations to gather the light and project it towards the interior.

FAZ ARMCHAIR
Vondom

The exercise of mineral faceting applied to a cube. The armchair looks like a stone case, yet it receives you comfortably on its upholstered seat and back. It is clearly not massive. Its very form tells you so, and the material confirms it. There is even an illuminated version that allows the armchair to be converted into a vaporous outdoor lamp.

One curious aspect is that although the facets might seem random, they are in fact measured to the millimetre, and the piece's symmetry demonstrates the orderly nature of its creation. From its appearance, all its different parts could have been faceted, but human symmetrical geometry finally overcame natural accidents and the whimsicality of form.

FAZ CARPET
Vondom

The gambit is to create a sensation of volume out of flatness by three means: an irregular outline, interior forms and different colours. These are really three different pentagons with irregular sides. Each shares only one side with its neighbours. The gradation of colours begins with the softest tone on the largest piece, drifts into brown, and ends with an uncompromising black, as though showing the shadows of each facet in the sun. Is architecture not the meeting of light and form, as Le Corbusier put it? Or, as Gaudí expressed it even better, 'architecture is the ordering of light; sculpture is the game of light'.

Peace and Comedy House

FAZ LOUNGER
Vondom

The entire Faz series is based on the faceting of planes to construct volumes. It is therefore an evolution of purist forms, a sort of deconstruction. Less rigid forms are sought, but without accepting the curve. The challenge is to solve this with planes, and the result is the creation of ridges, which are what produce the resulting aesthetic. It also has its precedents: Frank Lloyd Wright's Taliesin chair is shaped in this way, with plywood boards that nevertheless permit the intersection of planes. Now, with the help of the computer, the visibilisation and resolution of faceted forms are more practicable and refined.

The inspiration for this language, says the artist, is the crystallisation of minerals. However, although the origin may be organic, it refers us to abstraction, to the simplification of curves in planes. The effect achieved is the differentiated characterisation of each plane of light, all different due to the distinct angles of vision.

Owing to the flatness of its top, offering a greater contrast with its faceted base, the lounge chair is the pre-eminent piece in this collection. The three folds of the upper part harmonise with the set. Two—head and feet—are inclined, while the intermediate one is flat. It is very important to point out that there is nothing whimsical about these folds, as they are designed to ensure the necessary rigidity and occupy the smallest possible volume with the greatest expressive force.

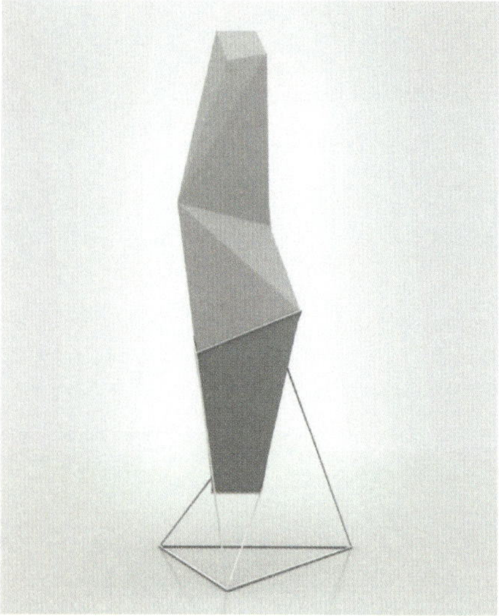

FAZ LAMP
Vondom

A naturally luminescent crystal. Or also a geometricised candle. Or a piece of phosphorescent ice. This is not a lamp but a luminous, weightless sculpture. Without a doubt, its great compositional achievement is to make it levitate. Resting on the ground, it would have been more banal. The subtle load-bearing structure is itself a dematerialised volume of which only the edges have remained, an unfaceted exoskeleton that explains the form mounted on it. The concept is one of great beauty and originality.

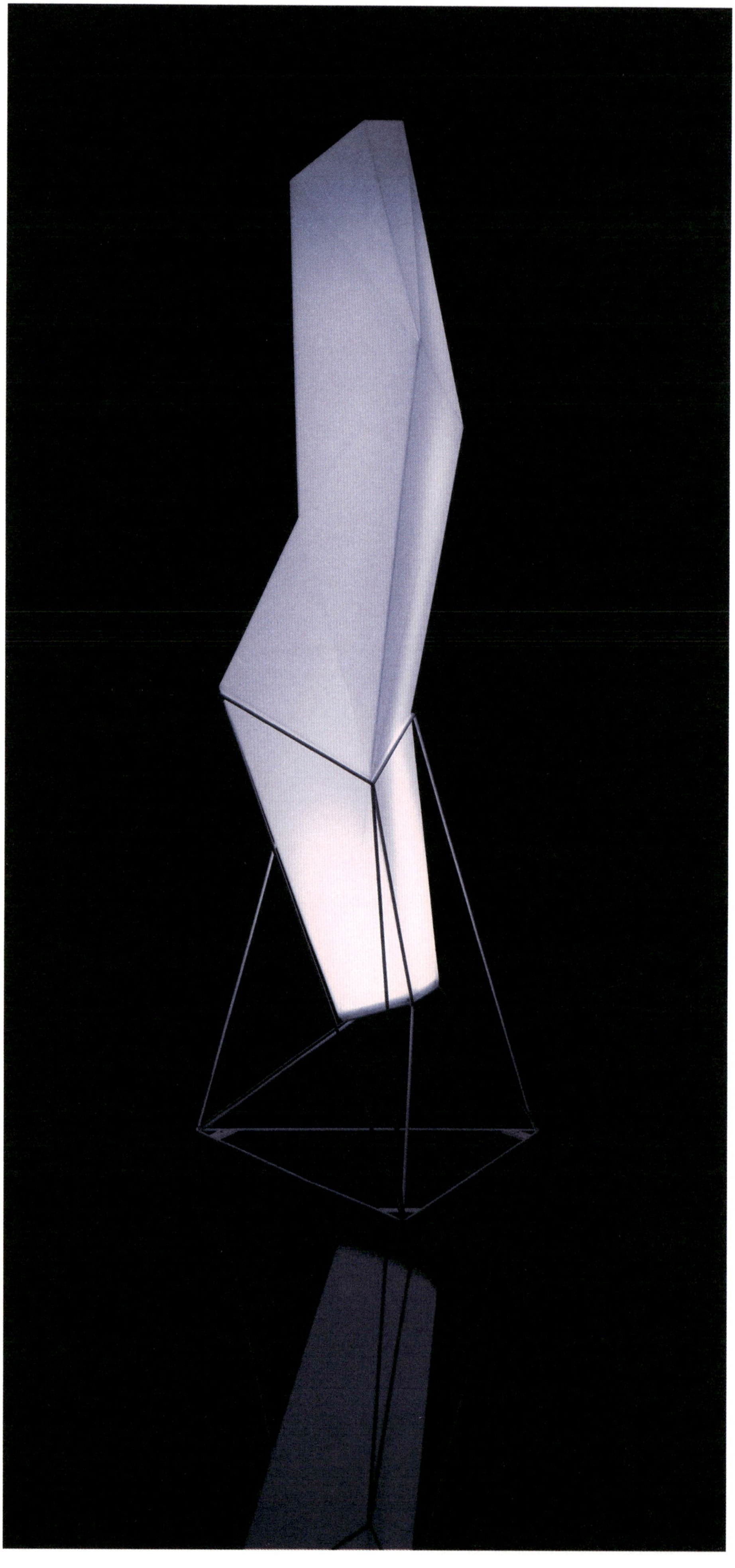

THE ESTABLISHMENT OF PARAMETERS, THE RESOLUTION AND THE WAY OF CONFRONTING AN OBJECT ARE NOT THE SAME AS WITH A BUILDING, BUT THE CONCEPTUALISATION CAN BE SIMILAR.

—

I LIKE CREATING AN *AUTEUR* DESIGN, BUT I WANT IT TO HAVE THE UNIVERSAL OR ESSENTIAL NATURE OF AN OBJECT THAT WASN'T THE WORK OF A DESIGNER, BUT WHICH BELONGS TO A CULTURE AND PROVIDES A SIMPLE SOLUTION FOR A NEED.

VELA
Vondom

'*Entrega*', or lodging, is a term Spanish-speaking architects use when two elements are brought together: one wins, the other wins, or a third is created to connect them. Here, we have an ambitious project to create a complete range of outdoor furnishing. This required a solid, simple and efficient base to be extended to the whole family of pieces. An orthogonal form that could be grouped, prolonged or turned around. Added to this rotund concept, however, is a significant gesture that makes it unique: lifting it off the ground. And here, this is not achieved with small interior legs or a recessed inner platform but with honesty, with the same material as is used to chamfer the side corners. The chamfer functions as a lodging, as a typical solution to a 90° angle, but also as material continuity. The visual perception changes radically: the mass no longer rests on the ground, whether lawn, paving or wood, but it is the ground that crawls under the furnishing. The image of solidity fades, and all the more if the furniture is illuminated.

An outstanding feature of this collection is the system for constructing outdoor bars. With three pieces—side, corner and door—it is possible to shape any composition. The bar surface becomes a fine skin of any material desired, like a tray for offering drinks and resting on. The break in the lower joint allows people to step precisely right up to the bar.

House in the forest

ENJOYING YOURSELF AND THINKING AND LETTING LIFE FLOW ON HAVE ALWAYS BELONGED TO THE MEDITERRANEAN CULTURE.

—

WE STILL LOOK FOR OBJECTS THAT WILL DRAW US TOWARDS THAT PURITY, WHICH ALSO HAS TO DO WITH THE SPIRITUAL DESIRE FOR EVERYTHING TO BE MUCH MORE ESSENTIAL.

—

I'M SOMEONE WITH A NATURAL TENDENCY TOWARDS THE ESSENTIAL, AND I SURROUND MYSELF WITH VERY FEW OBJECTS.

2011

Japan suspends whale-hunting / The first chapter of *Game of Thrones* is released on HBO / Mariano Rajoy is elected President of the Spanish government / Fidel Castro resigns as the First Secretary of the Communist Party of Cuba / Steve Jobs steps down as head of Apple.

CÓDIGO
De Castelli

The goal is to lighten the appearance of outdoor furniture. While it is usually heavy and massive, here it has successfully been made light and even transparent. The strategy for achieving this is to avoid both planes and volume. But then, what remains? The line. The thin vertical L-shaped structures comprise a subtle and dynamic framework. The reference to barcodes is implicit in the name of the collection, and the surprising result is the casting of expressive shadows.

This was the first collaboration with an international firm.

ELEMENTS
Inclass

Mass upon wires. The collection of chairs, tables and sofas is based once more on geometry, but far removed from purism, adding an irregular pattern of modulation. This avoids excessive solemnity and adds dynamism to the set. The powerful sofa, which rests on a light support structure, recalls a dematerialised volume marked only by the edges of a fine profile.

House in Rocafort

2013

Bicentennial of the birth of the composers Richard Wagner and Giuseppe Verdi / Jorge Mario Bergoglio becomes Pope Francis / First Airbus 350 flight.

FRAME
Vondom

After the disruptive Face collection, the time had come for a more relaxed but equally forceful outdoor furniture design. The result was this collection in polyethylene resin with rotational moulding that rests on the bevel edge of a frame, the leitmotif of the collection. This feature finds singular expression in the orthogonal joints, where the right angle makes not only for beauty but also for toughness and personality.

Special attention should be drawn to the fact that both the chair and the armchair are stackable, and also to the impressive design of the *chaise longue*, whose support surface seems to float between two empty frames.

House in Monasterios

FAZ DAYBED
Vondom

An interesting typological invention, this hybrid between a lounger and a pod is firmly bidding to become an icon. The piece forms part of the Faz collection, whose salient feature is the geometry of faceted gemstones. Here, the edges provide the whole piece with its volumetrics. The magic lies in the hood, like the lid of a treasured coffer, which not only provides shelter and shade but also, when closed, gives the piece the appearance of a rock. Moreover, it can incorporate loudspeakers activated by Bluetooth and a system of interior LED lighting. Truly galactic comfort.

Sardinera House

2014

King Juan Carlos I of Spain abdicates in favour of his son, Prince Felipe / Scotland holds a referendum on independence from the United Kingdom / The National Design and Innovation Awards, held since 1987, are not held this year.

VELA DAYBED
Vondom

This circular receptacle was designed to complete the Vela collection. The headpiece and footrest are reclinable, and it also hides an ice tray. It reminds us of a small inhabitable *tempietto* whose columns raise a protective fabric roof from which a delicate curtain hangs and swings in the breeze, protecting us from the sun and providing intimacy. The pure ancient essence of the Mediterranean with a contemporary resolution to evoke the height of relaxation.

ULM
Vondom

A clear tribute to the Ulm School, successor to the Bauhaus. Apart from its affable rationalism, the letter U itself ends up becoming the compositional element of this piece. The introduction of the curve allows both the seat and the back to present cushioning with curved ends, adding a sinuous touch to an overall design whose solid composition is thus toned down by a gesture familiar from Braun products.

2015

International Exposition in Milan / The Vatican recognises Palestine as a sovereign, independent nation / The New Horizons probe reaches Pluto / The United States reopens its embassy in Havana, Cuba.

ULM DAYBED
Vondom

The sketch of this piece suggests an open bivalve mollusc displaying a pearl inside. The base is composed as a truncated sphere whose interior is scooped out to form the comfortable upholstered area. A circular hood is then added, made from sun-protecting fabric, which serves when closed to protect the interior and provide visual order for the external space.

WHEN YOU WORK WITH SUCH ESSENTIAL FORMS, THE PROPORTIONS ARE THE MOST IMPORTANT THING OF ALL. THAT BALANCE IS VERY DIFFICULT TO ACHIEVE.

—

MY DESIGNS ARE ALWAYS BORN OF AN IDEA, A CONCEPT OR A SIMPLE DETAIL.

—

AN HONEST DESIGN, TO START WITH, IS ONE THAT IS FULLY FUNCTIONAL.

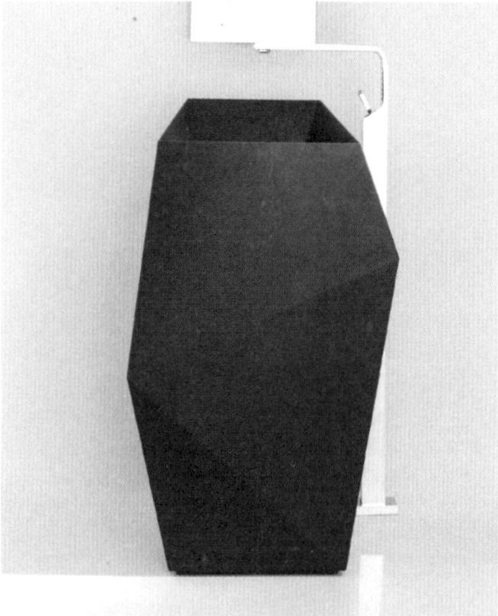

FACES
L'Antic Colonial

The language of facets developed in other designs is here applied to the bathroom, but this time using natural materials in the form of high-quality stones. It is then that the faceting becomes more committed, as it displays the veins and thus heightens precisely the mineral origin and monolithic geometrical structure of the stone. The most impressive piece is the vertical column of the basin, which looks like a menhir. As a complement, ceramic wall tiling, also faceted, has been designed in different models and finishes to allow highly expressive mural surfacing.

MINIM
L'Antic Colonial

An extensive wash basin collection with bathroom fittings in two different finishes: stone, to tone the bowl of the basin and the surrounding surface; and wood, which covers the furniture unit underneath. In both cases, the salient quality of the product is its flatness and elementary character. The attachment of the surface to the drawer, which leaves a subtle groove as an opening system, is one of the most successful details. A high-quality no-frills basin design that could sell forever.

House in La Pinada

P. 119

WHEN A BRAND HAS A VERY STRONG IDENTITY, IT MAKES IT MORE COMFORTABLE IN A CERTAIN WAY, BECAUSE PART OF THE PROCESS HAS ALREADY BEEN DONE FOR YOU.

—

A GOOD BRAND GIVES YOU A PRODUCT WHICH FITS INTO A COLLECTIVE THAT SEES THE WORLD IN A SIMILAR WAY OR IS EXCITED BY THE SAME THINGS. THERE'S A LANGUAGE, THERE'S A SERIES OF CODES IMPLICIT IN THE PIECE THAT CONNECT WITH A GROUP OF PEOPLE.

2016

Donald Trump wins the US presidential election / The circulation of autonomous cars is legalised in Europe / A earthquake measuring 7.0 on the Richter scale hits Japan / The WHO declares an international emergency due to the spread of the Zika virus / Bob Dylan receives the Nobel Prize for Literature.

KITCHEN COLLECTION
Gamadecor

The leap from furniture design to a full kitchen requires thorough prior training in spatial composition and a command of materials. However, it is easier for the practising architect, who is used to volumetric complexity. Here, moreover, the challenge is confronted in the sector of top-range kitchens aimed at a few select buyers. The collection was developed with six models: Ginger, Saffron, Cumin, Cinnamon and Pepper, all first-class culinary condiments. The bold and radical designs might be assimilated to architectural trends ranging from minimalism to high-tech and neo-vernacular, but there is one element that links them all together: the cantilever—the feat of making the surface hover without occupying any floorspace, defying constructive logic and introducing engineering to the kitchen.

CASILDA
Talenti

There is no doubt that it was the artist's reputation in the design of outdoor furnishings that persuaded the Italian firm Talenti, specialised in 'outdoor living', to contact him to create a new collection, thus joining other designers like Karim Rashid and Palomba+Serafini. The result is a complete collection that incorporates artisanal values which raise the category of the pieces. The sofa is composed of voluminous forms with an organic rather than geometrical nature, allowing a sewn casing that gives it a more informal appearance. The slats are visible, and interesting functional details are added, such as an extension for the armrest or a practical chairside table, like a corbel, because nearby support is always needed and hardly ever provided. There is also an interplay of wood and stone pieces in the material composition, one of the few decorative licences the designer permits himself.

CASILDA LAMPS
Talenti

Of all the accessories for the Casilda collection, special mention must go to these lamps. Seen from the front, they take the form of rectangles, but their base is given volume to create a solid support. Rising from this is a thin metal portico hiding a linear LED grid that outlines it with a warm glow. The iroko wood base matches that of the rest of the collection, and the small lamp goes equally well on a table or on the ground like a beacon.

2017

Centennial of the birth of John F. Kennedy / Space X launches a rocket with a reusable launch system / Banco Santander purchases Banco Popular for one euro / End of roaming in Europe / The Tour de France begins in Germany this year.

COTTAGE
Talenti

Inspired by the 'American far west, where armchairs with generous proportions and high backs inhabit the porches of farms and ranches', the main feature of this collection is the inclined structure in the form of an inverted V that supports the seat between the front and back legs. Its angle contributes dynamism to the piece, which looks as though it will bend when we sit on it. The central item in the set is the armchair with a high back, headrest and footrest module, which proudly displays its elegant 'corset' of broad slats behind it.

A CHAIR IS ALWAYS A CHALLENGE. TO GIVE IT AN IDENTITY, TO MAKE IT RECOGNISABLE, AND TO ENSURE IT'S NOT A PLAGIARISED VERSION OF SOMETHING ELSE IS VERY DIFFICULT.

—

IF YOU HAVE A BRIGHT IDEA, EVEN IF IT THEN PROVES DIFFICULT TO RESOLVE IT, YOU KNOW THAT'S WHAT'S GOING TO BE LEFT AT THE END.

—

IT MAY SEEM THAT WITH WOOD, METALS OR CERAMICS YOU ARE MORE LIMITED, BUT THEY GIVE YOU MORE CLUES. WITH PLASTIC THERE IS SO MUCH FREEDOM THAT IT GIVES YOU FEW CLUES.

KIMONO
Vondom

It has the elegance of a kimono, the subtlety of origami, the force of the mineral and the magic of transparency. It is a rotund, enigmatic and attractive chair. The central rhombus on the back, the compositional centre of the piece, creates a diamond-like effect. Thanks to its subtle faceting, different tonalities are created with every break in the plane. Although made from a single material, it looks like a compound surface. One of the most elegant, simplest and most expressive polycarbonate chairs on the market, it looks like a creature with an animate soul.

2018

The terrorist organisation ETA officially announces its dissolution / Pedro Sánchez becomes President of the government of Spain / Cristiano Ronaldo leaves Real Madrid / Women are allowed to drive in Saudi Arabia.

QUARTZ
Vondom

After trial runs with various collections of seats, the time had come to take the experimentation to its limit. This chair is a rigorous exercise in engineering and plasticity, and a meticulous synthesis of the two concepts. The sections are taken to the extreme with an injection of polyamide, a tough plastic that allows the most to be made of the material: 'A chair where every gram of material is justified.' The trick, nearly invisible, is to give the piece rigidity on the basis of folds, angles and triangulation. The frame of the back not only formalises a hollow volume but also characterises the piece by allowing it a subtle ergonomic curve for greater comfort. Its stackability, lightness, and universality make it an exercise in the best kind of extreme minimalism.

QUARTZ FOLDING CHAIR
Vondom

This is a revised and updated version of the traditional wooden folding chair but made in plastic, though avoiding the habitual form of plastic chairs. Added here is a regulator for adjusting the seat between the rear legs. The seat can be made more comfortable with a subtle curve, and it projects like a diminishing cantilever. The backrest is also curved for greater comfort. The toughness of the material allows for very fine components. Special mention should go to the delicate triangular detail of the swivel axis.

TABLET
Vondom

What would happen if we decomposed the basic volumetrics of a sofa? We would be left with parallelepipeds, lines and superimpositions. The objective of Tablet is to take furniture for sitting on to its highest degree of abstraction. The way to achieve this is to use a comfortable material, polyurethane foam, which turns rigid visual geometry into a pleasant support. The idea is for it to look hard but provide comfort. It is also like an elementary game with pieces of wood that allow you to reach infinity from a single module. The more elementary the piece, the more combinations, the greater the versatility, and the more infinite the possible arrangements. Another important quality is that it functions both outdoors and indoors, in homes and offices. The more basic the proposal, the greater the spatial adaptability. A single material, a single volume.

Llobatera House

TROCADERO
Talenti

Inspired by traditional Parisian café chairs, but with a shift towards compositional refinement. Everything is calibrated, even when the purpose is to make it look casual. For example, the vertical slats making up the seat-back unit, which are nevertheless positioned in two different widths with the apparently random broad/narrow rhythm 'BNBNNBN', give it a more informal and artisanal character. On the version with armrests, these are perfectly integrated with the aluminium tube, which in turn modifies its composition from round to square to receive the slats. A comfortable and welcoming chair with historic glamour.

LIGNAGE
Noken

For the spout of the tap, the goal is a perfect geometrical curve. In the large semicircle, the aerator at the end is not noticeable. For the handles, a simpler lever form is chosen rather than twist or ball heads. The characteristic detail is the grooving, which not only makes it comfortable to use precisely where it comes into contact with the user's wet and soapy hand but also decorates the piece with its linear texture.

It rests on a shield that not only hides the joint between body and base but also adopts a dignified conical form.

House in Rubielos de Mora

2019

'The best year in human history' according to *The New York Times* / The World Wide Web turns 30 / WikiLeaks founder Julian Assange is arrested in the embassy of Ecuador / Notre Dame cathedral catches fire.

GATSBY LAMP
Vondom

Come to the cabaret. More than a lamp, this is a 'heater' of tables and spaces. The name makes it clear that its inspiration comes from art deco and the 1920s, when parties were wild and glamorous. However, it is also a fine exercise in simplicity. Just three cylinders or parallelepipeds—base, trunk and lampshade—which, thanks to the grooved inner section, achieve a surprising effect. The pleated volumetric appearance has a transparency that makes it look lit even when switched off. However, when it is turned on in the darkness, its gleam explodes. It emits non-homogeneous rays, lighting the assembled company in an unusual way, and creates an effect of surprising patterns on the tablecloth or wall, rather like an illuminating kaleidoscope.

PIXEL
Vondom

The origin of this outdoor sofa is a highly significant original sketch: an orthogonal pattern of squares, like a crossword. However, as we are in the digital era, they are actually pixels—units that are identical despite their diverse finishes. Moving onto the project itself, it is composed of 1 × 1 m modules that embrace three possibilities: corner sofa, central sofa or pouffe. With this single element, it is possible to configure an infinite landscape, and suggestive colouring can also be added to either the polyethylene base or the upholstery, thereby effectively pixelating the space. The flatness of the set is emphasised by the low height of the seat, just 27 cm, which allows for the creation of a *décontracté* chillout space, as though we were lying on mats on the ground.

La Calma House

BLACK NOTE
LZF

At first sight, this lamp recalls a cylindrical candle, the archetype of traditional ceremonial lighting. However, it is a tube that is illuminated in its turn, displaying its organic vegetable texture when lit. In the linear version, the central axis is a light source pointing downwards, while the wall lamps distribute ambient light from what look like floating candles. This is a stylisation of the great candelabras of yesteryear, but with the subtlety of wooden casing and LED technology.

House in the garden

IN THE 20TH CENTURY THEY APPROACHED FURNITURE DESIGN FROM THE CONVICTION THAT IT IS NECESSARY FOR FURNISHINGS TO BE DEVELOPED COHERENTLY WITH THE SPACE THAT HOUSES THEM IF THE ARCHITECTURE IS TO YIELD ALL ITS SENSORY POTENTIAL.

—

FURNITURE ACTS AS A LINK BETWEEN A PLACE AND THE PERSON WHO LIVES IN IT, AMPLIFYING THE PERCEPTION OF THE EXPERIENCE OF INHABITING IT.

THESIS
LZF

Don't look for the bulb, as you won't find it. On a traditional standing or table lamp with a cylindrical shade, the question is how to hold the central bulb while hiding it at the same time. On this occasion, however, LED technology has allowed this classic type to be revisited with a magic trick. The lighting is set into the very structure that holds the lampshade. That is why the shade is so narrow, adding elegance to the piece. The structure is elementary: an efficient tripod at the base and another at the top, linked by a light central stem.

DESIGNING FURNITURE IS NOT THE SAME AS DESIGNING ARCHITECTURE. THE PARAMETERS ARE VERY DIFFERENT, AND EVERY PIECE OF FURNITURE IS A PROJECT. EVEN IF THE CONCEPTUALISATION IS THE SAME, THE REQUIREMENTS AND THE RESOLUTION ARE NOT.

—

THE ARCHITECT AND THE DESIGNER ARE LIKE AN ORCHESTRA CONDUCTOR, WHO KNOWS HOW TO MAKE USE OF THE RESOURCES, WHICH ARE THE MUSICIANS, BUT HAS TO KNOW FIRST HOW FAR A VIOLIN CAN GO OR HOW FAR A FLUTE CAN GO.

MOON DAYBED
Vondom

This time, the designer's preference for pure geometry has allowed him to experiment with the most potent of organic forms, the sphere. It is enough to cut it along a plane to be able to crawl inside and take shelter. This sphere is divided down the middle into two parts. The solid polypropylene base rotates to adapt to the movement of the sun and ensure the best views, while a perforated hood allows the pores to breathe but protects us from the sun.

A terrestrial capsule that plays at orbiting like the moon around the Earth, rather like a cocoon for disconnecting from the surroundings: a small oasis of rotating comfort.

Quarry House

2020

The United Kingdom implements Brexit and leaves the European Union / The WHO declares the COVID-19 pandemic.

ARPA
MDF Italia

As its name indicates, the collection is inspired by the strings of a harp. These are arranged as a motif that is functional as well as formal, as they support the side and back cushions. For greater emphasis, the design features a very fine structure and very plump, organic upholstery. Between the two, harmony is brought to the whole piece by thin strings, which are deliberately not arranged parallel to one another. A piece of musical furniture, light and graceful, that can go both indoors and outdoors.

House in La Finca

P.136

HUDSON
Danao Living

After years of trying out strong and radical designs, this piece represents the greater liberty of maturity. Without ties or restrictions, it employs forms and materials in absolute freedom. Stylistic harmony reigns. When seen from the rear, it exhibits belts and a leather strap forming a graceful armrest. It is also a continental leap for the designer, who, after working with producers in Valencia, started to collaborate in Italy with an American firm from New Jersey specialising in outdoor furnishings for its local market. With their organic and innovative forms, the pieces in this collection are inspired by American mid-century modern furniture, a post-war style with major contributions by designers like Saarinen, the Eames and Nelson, though they also display similarities with Italian *bel design*.

I'VE TRIED TO DO A *PRÊT-À-PORTER* BASED ON THE EXPERIENCE OF HAUTE COUTURE. THE PROMOTERS WANT IT, BUT THEY'RE NOT PREPARED TO SACRIFICE PROFIT IN RETURN FOR HIGHER QUALITY. AND THAT DOESN'T HAPPEN IN THE DESIGN INDUSTRY. THEY'RE MUCH MORE RECEPTIVE TO THAT CONCEPT OF A BRAND, A LIFESTYLE, THE SEGMENT AND THE CLIENT'S PHILOSOPHY.

—

IN DESIGN, WE WORK WITH *ROYALTIES*, WHICH IS A KIND OF ADVENTURE THAT INVOLVES SHARING THE SUCCESS WITH THE CLIENT. IT'S A FORMULA I'M HAPPY WITH. IN FACT, I'D LIKE IT TO HAPPEN WITH ARCHITECTURE AS WELL.

VINEYARD DAYBED
Vondom

The elementary refuge is a gabled roof. Minimal architecture. At the same time, however, it is the silhouette of the typical Valencian *barraca*, the dwelling whose overwhelming roof almost makes walls impossible. Here, we find two inclined planes in *deployé* or tensed cloth that shelter two loungers with reclining backs, creating small tables along the sides. It all floats on two subtle rectangular frames that raise the lower platform.

MY STUDIO IS WHERE I LIVE. IT'S A HOUSE AND STUDIO COMBINED.

—

THE IDEA IS TO PLAN A HANDOVER AND FORM A GROUP OF ASSOCIATES WHO WILL GRADUALLY TAKE OVER THE REINS.

—

I'M THE OLDEST IN EVERY WAY.

—

IT'S INTERESTING WHEN YOUNG PEOPLE PUT YOU IN CHECK, MAKING YOU GO WHERE YOU NORMALLY WOULDN'T, AND WHEN YOU GET THE CHANCE IN THE END TO TURN IT INTO SOMETHING SOLID. THAT WORKS.

CASILDA DAYBED
Talenti

The Casilda outdoor series is completed with this small piece of leisure architecture, which deliberately exaggerates the disproportion between the subtle structure and the soft upholstery of the base. It promises to be a luxurious den. The wind-blown curtains add a touch of lightness to an area of potent cushioning that guarantees comfort. It is complemented by the possibility of adding small side tables that are easily movable.

House in La Cañada

I'VE FITTED IN WITH CERTAIN FURNITURE PRODUCERS OR EDITORS BECAUSE I HAVE A FAIRLY SOBER, FAIRLY SERENE AND FAIRLY TIMELESS PHILOSOPHY. CREATING PIECES THAT SAY SOMETHING TO YOU AND ARE SO APPARENTLY NORMAL IS REALLY QUITE HARD. IT'S MUCH EASIER TO DIFFERENTIATE YOURSELF WITH SOMETHING EXCESSIVE.

MALTA
RH

An evocation of craftsmanship, with carefully managed joints and the magical textures of wood and plaited fibre. This collection concentrates the historicist criteria of Scandinavian and Italian chairs by cabinet maker designers, who aimed in the fifties and sixties at comfort and refinement. Every section of the armchair is geared towards enjoyment, seeking exactly the right measurements to guarantee resistance while remaining harmonious. Happily, optimum structure and gracefulness coincide.

CAICOS
RH

This is a design resolved by superimposing three horizontal layers. The first is the base, formed with a kind of support of metal beams that lift you off the ground. The second is the platform, constructed of teak wood slats placed on edge to provide the support. The last is the cushioned volumes, which are arranged according to the required function. Three different sediments for a relaxing territory that can be configured in countless ways.

Dels Vents House

2022

Valencia is named World Design Capital / Russia invades Ukraine / IKEA opens its first store in South America, in Santiago de Chile / The Football World Cup is held in Qatar / There are now 8 million people on Earth / Queen Elizabeth II dies.

VINEYARD
Vondom

Rolling boxes for mobile furniture. An appearance half-way between the colonial and the factory-made for nomadic, casual furnishings. The casings of wooden slats house the soft and comfortable upholstery. Sofas, armchairs, and large and small tables can wander around the space with their industrial wheels and create new compositions for the home.

Refuge in the vineyard

MITJORN
Isimar

With triangulated rods, it is possible to create sturdy structures with minimum girth and weight. They also give the piece a dynamic and graceful appearance. The legs are resolved with a turn at an acute angle, which gives them stability, and the armrests use a double rod to create a plane. Special mention goes to the prow-shaped angle of both the seat and the lounger, which adds a graceful marine touch.

I WAS AN ARCHITECTURE TEACHER FOR MANY YEARS, AND I USED TO RECOMMEND REPEATEDLY TO MY STUDENTS THAT THEY SHOULD LEARN ABOUT PROCESSES TO AVOID BECOMING CARETAKERS OF CATALOGUES AND PATENTS INVENTED BY OTHERS. EVEN IF YOU USE THEM LATER ON, IT'S IMPORTANT TO GET TO KNOW THEM IN DEPTH AND TO QUESTION THEM SO AS TO BE ABLE TO COME UP WITH DIFFERENT RESULTS.

TEMPO
Alexandra Forwards

In its catalogue, the firm Alexandra offers three different sectors united by a search for maximum quality and comfort. One is classic furniture, the second is contemporary furnishing, and the third, the Forwards collection, offers modern pieces with a classical vocation. This is the home of Tempo, an ambitious programme of sofas, tables, sideboards and chairs with timeless forms and materials.

GATSBY
Vondom

In the beginning was the light. Indeed, the inspiration for this collection came from the Gatsby lamp designed in 2019, a century after the blossoming of art deco, whose fluted glass with golden glints tried to evoke the glamorous twenties. It proved to be such a powerful formal icon that it has given rise years later to a system of sofas that guarantee comfort while offering the possibility of a sensual new curved layout. Also added are tables and plant stands whose distinctive feature is their vertical fluting. These are pieces that could fit well in any voluptuous art deco interior.

The Rock House

THE FACTORY
Vondom

Cut and stretched metal—that is, *deployé*—was born as a quick and cheap solution for transparent closures, replacing the more complex soldered grilles. In the 1970s, however, Clotet and Tusquets were bold enough to turn it into a comfortable material for furniture with their Catalano bench. Since then, it has acquired another expressive dimension, which in The Factory is sophisticated enough to contribute elegance and glamour. The moiré creates an optical effect that adds to the graphic potency projected by the shadow of the material. Its lightness contrasts with a great mass of cushioning, an opposition that shapes the collection.

LARGE
Lebom

A design to complement the catalogue of the Valencian firm Lebom, created in 2019. Its collection was missing a large and ambitious piece ready to conquer luxurious territories and broad spaces. Thanks to a subtle platform, almost a cantilever with its support barely visible, the Large composable system allows a complete configuration of the space it furnishes.

Olea House

THE CREATIVE PROCESS ISN'T LINEAR, ALTHOUGH WE NARRATE IT IN A LINEAR FASHION.

—

YOU DON'T NECESSARILY HAVE TO PRODUCE AN EASILY RECOGNISABLE LINE, BUT THERE MUST BE A PERCEPTIBLE HARMONY AND CONTINUITY WHEN YOU PUT ALL THE PRODUCTS TOGETHER.

—

WHEN YOU START TO DESIGN, WHAT YOU WANT IS TO DEVELOP YOUR OWN CREATIVE UNIVERSE.

JUMBO
Lebom

From the front, it looks like a Corinthian column. The expression of this piece is entrusted to the back, a perfect cylinder of generous proportions. By turning the corner to become an armrest, it displays its radical concept. Two circles that function like a magnet, attracting people to sit down on it.

2023

Year of the Rabbit according to the Chinese calendar / Coronation of King Charles III of the United Kingdom / Milano Design Week and the Salone del Mobile are once again benchmarks for design professionals.

DAYBED IGLU
Vondom

In the wake of having virtually invented the concept of the daybed, an even more difficult challenge presented itself. After testing with cylinders, circles, parallelopipeds and two slopes came this proposal which perfectly summarises micro-architecture. The geodesic dome, developed by the visionary Buckminster Fuller, is capable of covering the space with lightweight structures based on triangular edges. The effect looks futuristic and evokes a spherical volume broken into diamonds whose interior serves as a retreat.

HAMPTONS
Vondom

He has had more than 100 pieces in the Vondom Esteve catalogue since his first collaboration in 2010. Even so, it is possible to add new ones of interest every now and then. In this case, the challenge is to give shape to a hypothetical sofa for summer luxury summery homes. The main inspiration is the Hamptons, the area on Long Island where New York's wealthy class passes its vacations. It features a subtle cylindrical structure, a reference to striped awnings and white-edged, oversized cushions where it would be easy to imagine the Great Gatsby lounging. Yet it would also fit in perfectly in a mansion on the French Riviera, the retreat of choice of Europe's jet set.

Clos de la Villa House

HAYDEN
Bolia

Scandinavian design comes not only from the Swedish company IKEA but also from other more sophisticated brands, like the Danish company Bolia, which focuses on traditional Nordic comfort and look and feel. Its expansion strategy, with the goal of opening in Spain with its own shop in Barcelona in 2023, sought to include a few Esteve pieces to give its collections a more Mediterranean feel. The Hayden sofa delivers this mixture of Nordic organicity and a more informal, sensual Latin touch. Its legs stand out; they seem to have escaped from the upholstery to show their ligneous material nature.

POSIDONIA
Vondom

Back to basics. The Posidonia collection closes the circle started in 1996, when Esteve decided to create a collection of outdoor furnishings to match the interior aesthetics of his single-family home in Ibiza. That was the birth of Na Xemena, a line of furnishings whose concept is now revived, though formalised in a striking new way, and christened with the name of the algae that give the Mediterranean its life. The collection is dazzling, with a total of 42 pieces forming a complete repertoire for fitting out a terrace with the same look as any timeless and permanent interior. In this curious pirouette, with a beginning and end that coincide, a repertoire remains in between of nearly three decades of experimenting with the 'isms' of international architecture. In the end, it is the essence that remains.

TEAM

RAMÓN ESTEVE STUDIO

In the image,
from left to right:

Eva Giral (designer)
Carlos Granell (designer)
Nacho Poveda (director of the Design Department)
Ramón Esteve
Juan Ferrero (CEO)
Gloria Izquierdo (senior designer)
Natalia Fonseca (director of the Administration and Finance Department)

Contributors:

Carlos Real
Pablo Verdes

Silvia Martínez
Isabel Meyer
Tudi Soriano

Isabel Rojo
Tania López
Aldo Bertomeu

Julia Ballesteros
Alejandra Centelles
Álex Pérez
Patricia Clemente
Ana Llobet

THIS IS NOT A HOUSE.
RAMÓN ESTEVE

Publisher:
La Fábrica

Editorial Direction:
Ramón Úbeda

Graphic Designer:
Formo

Texts:
Juli Capella

Conversations between Ramón Esteve and Juli Capella, Quique Dacosta, Antxón Gómez, Tachy Mora and Alberto Anaut, conducted by Ramón Úbeda

Editorial Coordinator:
Miriam Querol

Translations:
Philip Sutton

Proofreading:
Art in Translation

Documentation:
Carla Bayo, Laura Murcia, Nacho Poveda and Juan Ferrero

Photographs:
Paco Alberca, Fernando Alda, Mariela Apolonio, Alfonso Calza, Servando Carmona, Josele Castellón, Léa Chave, Cuality Photo Studio, Javier Biosca, Chencho Duato, Ramón Esteve, Xavi Gordo, Christoph Kicherer, Xavi Molla, Eduardo Peris, Mayte Piera, Eugeni Pons, Santiago Relanzón, RH, Sara Sánchez, Jonathan Segade, Ángel Segura, Mario Sierra and Ferran Val

Every effort has been made to identify the authors of the images. Any error or accidental omission will be rectified in subsequent editions.

Production:
Adriana Rodríguez

Digital image:
Quatre Caps and Cru Atelier

Printers:
Brizzolis, arte en gráficas

LA FABRICA

Founder:
Alberto Anaut

Director:
Óscar Becerra

Publishing Director:
César Martínez-Useros

Editorial Content Manager:
Camino Brasa

Distribution Manager:
Raúl Muñoz

ISBN: 978-84-18934-75-9
Legal deposit: M-24736-2023

La Fábrica
C/ Alameda, 9
28014, Madrid
T. +34 91 360 13 20
www.lafabrica.com

Ramón Esteve Estudio
Plaça de Pere Borrego i Galindo, 7. Bajo
46003 València
T. +34 96 351 04 34
www.ramonesteve.com